This is the ABYSSINIAN CAT

KATE FALER

*Dedicated to Abys the world over and to two
special cats: Querdia's Poco Bueno of Bromide,
my first Aby, and Bazoona, my first cat.*

Photography
Andrea Zaun Balcerski: 162 (top), 163 (top); Ruth Bauer: 24, 29 (top),
120, 132 (top), 138, 144, 145 (top), 147 (top); Jeanclaire Bridgers: 38,
29; Philip Channing: 149; Bob Chorneau: 143 (bottom); Rae Ann
Christ: 113; Jim Cooper: 147 (bottom); Donna Coss: 146 (bottom),
156; Jal Duncan: 40-1, 48, 117, 125; Karl Faler: 46, 52, 53, 62, 63, 64-5,
66-7, 68, 69, 71, 80, 99 (left), 102, 106, 111, 178, 179, 181, 182, 183;
Lewis Fineman: 17, 34, 36, 37, 44 (bottom), 47, 49, 74, 116, 128 (top),
168, 174; Jane Howard: 160; J'Sen's: front cover, 20, 25, 136-7, 139
(bottom), 145 (bottom); Kevin Mahoney: 124, 133; Robert Pearcy: 33;
Vincent Serbin: 9, 51, 54, 56, 83, 88 (top), 90, 96, 98, 99 (right), 115;
Mrs. Pat Sheumack, 163 (bottom); Dr. Henrietta N. Shirk: 43, 176; Bill
Smith: 6; Lew Soper: 15; Alice Su: 162 (bottom); Bob Taylor: 55;
Elaine Thieroff: 139 (top), 150, 155; John Turner: 10, 22-3 28 (bottom),
42-3, 45 (bottom), 112 (top), 118, 132 (bottom), 140 (top), 141, 143
(top), 164, 171, 172-3, 177; Scott Van Dugor: 129; Joan Wastlhuber:
back cover, 5, 28 (top), 29 (bottom), 33, 42, 44 (top), 45 (top), 112 (bottom), 120, 128 (bottom), 140 (bottom), 170; Jim Zimmermann: 88 (bottom); Ruth Zimmermann: 76-7, 100, 105, 107, 108, 109.

Front cover: Gr. Ch. El Qahira's Deseret. Breeder/owner: Rae Ann
Christ.

Back cover: A basketful of beautiful five-week-old female Nepenthes kittens. Breeders/owners: Joan and Alfred Wastlhuber.

Title page: Intelligent, graceful, and dignified, Abyssinians have
won the hearts of cat lovers everywhere.

*The portrayal of feline pet products in this book is for general instruc-
tive value only; their appearance does not necessarily constitute an
endorsement by either the author or publisher.*

"The History of the Abyssinian Cat" chapter, which is composed of
excerpts from an article written by Dr. Rosemonde S. Peltz for the
1972 CFA *Yearbook*, has been reprinted with permission from the
Cat Fanciers' Association, Inc.

t.f.h.

Distributed in the UNITED STATES by T.F.H. Publications, Inc., 211 West
Sylvania Avenue, Neptune City, NJ 07753; in CANADA by H & L Pet Supplies
Inc., 27 Kingston Crescent, Kitchener, Ontario N2B 2T6; Rolf C. Hagen Ltd.,
3225 Sartelon Street, Montreal 382 Quebec; in ENGLAND by T.F.H. (Great
Britain) Ltd., 11 Ormside Way, Holmethorpe Industrial Estate, Redhill, Sur-
rey RH1 2PX; in AUSTRALIA AND THE SOUTH PACIFIC by T.F.H. (Australia)
Pty. Ltd., Box 149, Brookvale 2100 N.S.W., Australia; in NEW ZEALAND by
Ross Haines & Son, Ltd., 18 Monmouth Street, Grey Lynn, Auckland 2 New
Zealand; in SINGAPORE AND MALAYSIA by MPH Distributors Pte., 71-77
Stamford Road, Singapore 0617; in the PHILIPPINES by Bio-Research, 5
Lippay Street, San Lorenzo Village, Makati, Rizal; in SOUTH AFRICA by
Multipet Pty. Ltd., 30 Turners Avenue, Durban 4001. Published by T.F.H.
Publications Inc., Ltd., the British Crown Colony of Hong Kong. THIS IS
THE 1983 EDITION.

Contents

ABOUT THE AUTHOR

Kate Faler and her husband Karl have been raising Abyssinians for over ten years, and have taught college veterinary technology classes. She has a B.S. in bacteriology, a masters degree in biology education, and is currently a veterinary student at Washington State University (D.V.M.-in 1985). Kate is a founding member of The Abyssinian Breeders of the Cascades, member of the Abyssinian Cat Club of America and CFA Breed Council. Her Bromide Cattery has bred several grand champions.

ABOUT THE CONTRIBUTORS

Kim Everett

Kim Everett is a CFA all-breed judge and a member of the CFA National Board of Directors. She and her husband (also a CFA all-breed judge) own Pharoh and Swingate Catteries. They have bred white, blue, blue-cream, and cream Persians, as well as their specialty, Abyssinians, having produced some of the greatest Abys of all time. Included among her cats were two "Cats of the Year" in 1966 and 1973. She organized the first CFA cat club in the Northwest—The Oregon Cat Fanciers, Inc. Kim is also a member of Professional Aby Breeders and is active in local CFA clubs. She has written articles for *Cat World*, *All Cats*, and *Cat Fancy* magazines.

Wain Harding

Wain Harding has bred cats for fourteen years and Abyssinians for nine of those years. His cattery name is Bastis, and it has produced twelve Aby grand champions. Wain is secretary for the Abyssinian Cat Club of America and is a shorthair judge in CFA.

Kenna L. Mawk

Kenna L. Mawk graduated in 1972 from the University of Arizona with a B.S. in nutritional science. In 1976, she obtained her Doctor of Veterinary Medicine from Washington State University. Currently practicing in San Jose, California, she breeds and shows Abyssinians under the cattery name of Kenalee.

4

Rosemonde S. Peltz

Dr. Rosemonde Peltz owns Heatherwood Cattery, where she breeds, ASH, Exotic Shorthairs, Scottish Folds, and American Wirehairs. She holds degrees in fine art and medicine. Dr. Peltz has a private practice of internal medicine and cardiology in Decatur, Georgia and is a medical consultant to the state of Georgia. For 10 years she served as a CFA board member and has contributed articles to various cat publications throughout the world.

Jeannette Walder

Jeannette Walder has been breeding and showing Abyssinians since 1972 under the cattery name of Helium. Her primary interest is red Abyssinians, but she also has ruddies, a blue Persian and a brown tabby ASH. She is currently editor of the Abyssinian Cat Club of America newsletter, and former editor of the Abyssinian Midwest Breeders newsletter. She is a CFA shorthair specialty judge and an attorney by profession.

Patricia Nell Warren

Patricia Nell Warren is past president of the International Somali Cat Club and was CFA's 1979-81 Somali breed secretary. She has written on the breed for *Cats, All Cats, Cat World, Cat-Tab, CFA Yearbook, The Abyssinian Cat, Katten Vär, Cats/Canada/Chats*, and other publications.

Joan Wastlhuber

Joan Wastlhuber, with her husband Alfred, obtained her first Abyssinian in 1969 and began breeding in 1971. She has now bred 14 CFA grand champions and three grand premiers, including four CFA National Award winners. In addition to her Abys, she owns a 13 year old brown classic tabby American Shorthair grand premier and two blue Persian females. She is the CFA Abyssinian Breed Council Secretary, President of the Robert H. Winn Foundation for Cat Research, and the Abyssinian panel member for the Jane Martinke Reference Center. She is a CFA shorthair judge and a member of The San Francisco Revelers, Inc., Poppy State Cat Club, Abyssinian Cat Club of America, and Western Abyssinian Cat Club. Joan and her husband own Nepenthes Cattery, which was covered in the September/October 1978 issue of *Cat World* magazine and the April/May 1981 issue of *All Cats* magazine. Nepenthes has been visited by people from all over America as well as from many foreign countries and it has been acclaimed as an outstanding environment for breeding cats. She is an interior designer and art consultant by profession.

Two litters of Nepenthes kittens cuddle up for a group photograph. Half were the product of a Gr. Ch. Nepenthes Cysko and Golden Ra Majesta of Nepenthes mating. The other half also were sired by Cysko out of Ch. Nepenthes Pride 'n Joy of Valley. Breeders/owners: Joan and Alfred Wastlhuber.

Gr. Pr. Amara Red Rollei of Will-Ane, a red male.
Breeder: Lorna B. Malinen. Owners: Bill and Pat
Smith and Lorna B. Malinen.

PREFACE

The cat fancy consists of people from all walks of life, and one of the delights of cat shows is to meet people with a variety of backgrounds, careers, and attitudes. The Abyssinian breed has many devoted people working with it, and it is a privilege to associate with them. Some of the fanciers who have expertise in certain aspects of the breed have contributed sections to this book. All who love Abys will be most grateful to them for sharing their knowledge with us.

This book is oriented towards the Cat Fanciers' Association, Inc. (CFA), the largest, as well as one of the oldest, cat registries in the United States today. About 90% of all U.S. cats are registered with CFA, which has almost double the total show entries of all other associations combined (*Cats* magazine, September 1977). It would have been a monumental task to include information from all of the associations, so it seemed appropriate to concentrate on CFA. It is hoped readers who are not interested in CFA will be able to infer the information they need.

Currently, only ruddy and red Abyssinians have championship status in CFA. Blues may be registered in CFA as A.O.V. (any other variety Abyssinians), and it is for this reason that they are not dealt with in this book. Interest in this "new" color (actually, blues have been bred for a number of years now) has increased steadily in the past few years, and we can hope the future will bring a resolution to the question of whether blue Abys are a hybrid or a naturally occurring color.

The Abyssinian's steady growth in popularity took a large leap with the release of Walt Disney's movie *A Cat From Outer Space*, which starred an Abyssinian. One of the best ways to make sure that the breed improves rather than declines in purity and beauty as a result of this popularity is to educate newcomers to the fancy. One of the major purposes for this book is the protection of the breed that will come with the new respect gained through knowledge of its history, care, and potential.

I hope the inclusion of controversial material or the exclusion of what others may regard as pertinent information gives no offense.

I thank most gratefully my guest authors, my husband, my father (who gave me much guidance), Tom Dent at CFA, Lynn Steffen who encouraged me, and all those cat people who answered my letters and returned the surveys.

Suggestions and comments by readers are most welcome.

Kate Faler
Bromide Cattery

Introduction

This book is designed for Abyssinian admirers of all types. It includes information of interest to investigators, pet owners, novice breeders, experienced breeders, and general cat fanciers, as much of the information can be applied to other breeds as well.

Abyssinians are unique among domestic cats in terms of their coat, color, and pattern. Their fur is composed of the characteristic "agouti ticking," a pattern that occurs when each individual hair is banded with color. There are only two color varieties accepted for championship by CFA, ruddy and red. The hair of ruddy Abyssinians has bands of black alternating with a rusty-red color, while the hair of red Abyssinians has brown bands which alternate with the same rusty-red color. The tail tip and paw pads of the ruddy are black. The red has a brown tail tip and pink-rose paw pads. The face in both colors has delightful tabby markings which outline the eyes and give an individual expression to each cat. The eyes are usually a rich gold, but they may also be green. The nose leather is brick red in the ruddy and pink in the red.

The entire appearance of an Abyssinian is like that of a miniature cougar or other wild cat. (My home contains the pelt of a cougar shot by a family member generations ago. When visitors come to see my Abyssinians, I often hold one against the cougar pelt, and the resemblance is truly amazing!) This feral appearance makes them especially appealing to men. Abys are good alternatives for those who want to own an exotic cat but do not wish to have the problems that are associated with undomesticated animals. Agouti ticking (see Genetics chapter) is found on a number of other wild animals besides cougars, including deer, squirrels, rabbits, mice, elk, and so forth.

Personality varies from cat to cat; no two are exactly alike. However, one of the advantages of owning a purebred animal is being able to predict what the offspring will be like, based on its ancestors. Included in the breeder survey conducted for this book was a request for a few adjectives that described the Abyssinian. The following list resulted, and the words are listed in order from most commonly used to those mentioned at least twice. It is hoped that a picture of the Aby personality can be drawn from these descriptive words.

Two of the Aby's most striking features are its beautiful ticked coat and its dramatic facial markings that give this elegant feline its sweet, expressive look.

intelligent	possessive	beautiful
(very) affectionate	people-oriented	unique
playful	water-loving	fascinating
active	elegant	determined
alert	graceful	bold
inquisitive	quick	sensitive
clever	responsive	trusting
quiet	intuitive	mischievous
gentle	busy	sympathetic
out-going	regal	sweet
personable	self-assured	friendly
lively	loyal	kittenish
clean	perceptive	trainable
curious	independent	captivating

Abyssinians shower their owners with love and attention. They insist on being included in all projects, especially wallpapering, knitting, and small repairs. Abys thrive on lap-sitting, nose-rubbing, and bed-sleeping. They are very sensitive to people's moods. They are comforting when their owner is lonely, sick, or unhappy and joyous when all is well. One of their most endearing qualities is their soft little voices which express their feelings quite well. Meeting life with zest and a sense of humor, they enrich the lives of all they come in contact with. Everyone should be owned by an Aby at some time in his or her life.

History of the Abyssinian Cat

by Rosemonde S. Peltz

Abyssinians are a special type of tabby cat; they are distinguished from all other tabbies by their beautiful ticked, resilient coats. All tabbies, in fact, have this ticked or agouti background in their coats (whereby each individual hair shaft is banded with different colors); however, superimposed on this ticked background is a particular dark pattern such as mackerel, spotted, or blotched. Through more than 85 years of selective breeding, these dark patterns have been nearly eliminated from the Abyssinian breed, and this is what makes them so unique. Although other tabbies are bred in different colors, Abyssinians are bred and recognized for championship by CFA only in the ruddy and red varieties.

Some breeders prefer to believe that Abyssinians are the most ancient of breeds and that they were both companions and gods of the Egyptians. The history of the Abyssinian breed could begin wherever a ticked tabby walked, because similar cats existed in all countries. The notion that ticked cats were imported here, there, and everywhere is a rather provincial idea. There is little or no doubt that Abyssinian cats developed in England, for there is no record of any Abyssinian cat imported there.

Like so many other breeds, the Abyssinian is not without its legends, but the truth of the matter is that the Abyssinian is more at home on the Thames than on the Nile. The British really hand-tailored a group of cats that they called Abyssinians. They began with what was at hand, the British Shorthairs; many of these cats were of unknown parentage. That is not to say that a ticked cat did not come upon the scene to be used in the program; the earliest records indicate that the main requirement for the breed was a ticked coat. In the beginning, there was a great range of colors, extending from the wild silver agouti ticking to an intense yellow ticking. The silver color

Pictured is Gr. Ch. Anshent-won Anahita. Breeders/owners: Dr. and Mrs. John W. Boyd (Joyce Chang).

11

seems to predominate in the early Abyssinians if one notices the names of the cats. Such names as Aluminum, Quicksilver, Silver Memelik, and Silver Fairy hardly could have been given to ruddy-colored cats. Today, breeders are concerned about a silver "mutation," and such concern takes on another perspective in light of the early colored Abyssinians. Mr. H.C. Brooke (one of the early British breeders) opposed the silver color and, in order "to get back the warmth of body color . . .," used a cat he described as a "self red" in breeding his cats (Denham and Denham, 1951).

In the beginning, Abyssinians were, thus, silver cats accompanied by remnants of tabby markings. At a time when silver and brown tabbies were truly popular in England, breeders tried to produce a totally distinctive cat. They introduced a little red to warm up the coat as Mr. Brooke did, and they bred out the tabby markings. This kind of work took a long time and required great effort.

When any breed is established, there are certain breeders' names and cats that dominate the early registrations. Among those very early Abyssinian breeders were Mrs. Constance Carew-Cox, Miss E.A. Clarke, Mrs. Frederick, Mrs. Patman, Lady Edith Douglas-Pennant, and Lady Decies. Two other important names were Mr. Sam Woodiwiss and Mr. H.C. Brooke. All of these people were significant breeders of their time and they are responsible for establishing the Abyssinian as a recognized breed.

The first Abyssinian registrations occurred in 1896, and the stud book of the National Cat Club reveals that Sedgemere Bottle, born in 1892, and Sedgemere Peaty, born in 1894, were registered by Mr. Sam Woodiwiss. Peaty had been previously owned by a Mr. Swinyard and later was acquired by Mr. Brooke (Denham and Denham, 1951).

In the 1900-1905 stud books, 12 Abyssinians, each of which had one or both parents listed as unknown, were registered. In 1903, a particularly fine female named Fancy Free was born. There was also a male born July 13, 1905 that was named Aluminum. These cats were bred and owned by Mrs. Carew-Cox, and they appear in many of the early pedigrees. Mr. and Mrs. Denham's book, *Child of The Gods*, indicates Fancy Free was silver and won the Abyssinian championship cup at the Westminster Show of 1909. Fancy Free and Aluminum produced a fine male kitten named Aluminum II. He was born on September 2, 1907, and was acquired by Miss J.R. Cathcart of the United States. Miss Cathcart also obtained another cat, a female named Salt. According to Mrs. Zanetti (Zanetti, Dennis, and Hantzmon, 1906), Aluminum II and Salt were the first imports to the United States.

Of course, World War I caused considerable delay in the establishment of the Abyssinian cat as a recognized breed in the United States. The nucleus of the new breed was small, not only in the United States, but also in Britain. There is no record of later imports until Virginia Cobb of Newton Cattery registered Woodroofe Ena of Newton, a female, born in December, 1933. Ena had been bred by Major Sydney Woodiwiss. Virginia Cobb also acquired Woodroofe Anthony from Major Woodiwiss. From this pair of cats came Djer-Mer's Melikot of Newton and Djer-Mer's Yeshe Imabet of Newton. This male and female were born on June 23, 1936 and bred by Virginia Cobb. Mrs. Martin Metcalfe and Mary Hantzmon later obtained these kittens.

The great efforts of Mrs. Metcalfe of Drexel Hill, Pennsylvania and Ms. Hantzmon of Washington, D.C. brought about the final establishment of the Abyssinian as a recognized breed in the United States. (It should be noted that cattery names can be confusing to the novice, as the practices and rules of cattery names have changed over the years. As has been indicated, the breeder of the above kittens, Melikot and Yeshe Imabet, was Virginia Cobb of Newton Cattery; however, Mrs. Metcalfe and Ms. Hantzmon of Djer-Mer Cattery consistently use Djer-Mer as a *prefix*, even on imported cats). The next cat that Djer-Mer obtained was a male, Ras Seyum, from Major Woodiwiss. Those readers who have access to the November, 1938 issue of *National Geographic* magazine can see a picture of that cat, Djer-Mer's Woodroofe Ras Seyum. These two women continued to import Abys from England; the next two imports were females, Djer-Mer's Croham Isana and her litter sister, Djer-Mer's Croham Justina, born on April 3, 1938. They were bred by Mrs. C. Basnett.

Ten Djer-Mer Abyssinian kittens were registered in volume 19 of the *Stud Book Register* of the Cat Fanciers' Association. Interestingly, each of these cats was sired by Ras Seyum and the dam was Yeshe Imabet in seven of the ten registrations. That year Mrs. Metcalfe and Ms. Hantzmon also registered a cat bred by Mrs. Gardner Fiske named Djer-Mer's Zelasse. This female kitten was born in July, 1935, and was the product of the early imports Woodroofe Anthony and Woodroofe Ena of Newton. Zelasse was the dam of three kittens. At that time the women decided to share their good stock with other breeders, and five kittens went to breeders in Pennsylvania, New York, Michigan, and, Ohio.

Just when the period of intensive breeding began in the United States in 1938 to 1939, the great tragedy of World War II occurred. By the end of the war, only 12 or so Abyssinians were left in England, and this certainly hampered breeding efforts here in the United States.

Between 1945 and 1946, Helen Fairchild, Robert Richardson, and Mildred Alexander were breeding Abyssinians in the United States. The popularity of the breed was furthered here by a lovely book called *Cats and All About Them* written by Dr. and Mrs. Fairchild. In it there are several pictures of the imports Djer-Mer's Woodroofe Myoa and Woodroofe's Mira.

Two female kittens bred by Lady Barnard and born on May 21, 1948, were acquired by Blanche Warren of California. These were Raby Nefertari and Raby Aida. Their sire was Raby Ashanto and their dam Wagphur Cleopatra. Raby Ramphis of Disston was the litter brother and went to Mrs. T.A. Kloos. This cat was later transferred to Mrs. Gaston Comhaire of Texas. Next, Mrs. Kloos imported Merkland Sheba of Disston who had been born on May 29, 1948. This cat was sired by Kreeoro Kaffa and had been bred by Lord and Lady Liverpool. From 1947 to 1949, the principal breeders of Abyssinians in this country were Alice Archibald, Gaston Comhaire, and Robert Richardson.

In 1949, Frances Schuler Taft began her extraordinary career with Abyssinians. Mrs. Taft acquired her first Abyssinian when she bought a male from Blanche Warren. Later on she obtained Caper Cat Trinket and Caper Cat Idyllwild from Judy Smith of New York.

Judy Smith imported Pussner Pride and Pussner Paragon to improve the stock in her Caper Cat Cattery. Pride had been bred by Lady Hedlam and had been born on June 18, 1949. The sire was Raby Ashanto. The dam of this kitten was Pussner Cat. Pussner Paragon, born a month earlier, On May 21, 1949, had been sired by Kreeoro Kaffa. Its dam was Straw.

Blanche Warren imported another male sired by Kreeoro Kaffa. The cat, Merkland Habesh De Casa Gatos, had been bred by Lord and Lady Liverpool and had been born on March 26, 1949. The dam of Habesh was Merkland Telari, sired by Raby Ashanto. In addition, Blanche Warren also acquired the litter sister named Merkland Magdala.

The Hoeller Cattery had been established by Kathleen and Paul Hoeller, and they imported a male and female of the same litter that had been born August 7, 1949. This litter had been bred by Lord and Lady Liverpool. The cats were named Hoeller's Merkland Dembea, a female, and Hoeller's Merkland Takazza, a male.

Abyssinian breeders increased in numbers; in 1950, the list of Aby breeders included Winifred Porter of New Orleans. Mrs. Porter acquired a cat from Ms. C. Basnett. This was The Farm's Croham Zena. This female Abyssinian, born April 27, 1950, had been sired by Croham Abeba. Mrs. Porter also imported another female sired by Croham Abeba, The Farm's Nigella Mimi, that had been born April 9, 1950, and had been bred by Ms. F.A. Bone. Kreeoro Kaffa had sired the dam of Mimi, and that cat was Merkland Adowa.

By 1951, the group of Abyssinian breeders expanded even more. Joining them was Isabel Allen, Beth O'Donovan, and Van Estes. In 1952, Bob Forrest, LaVona Wright, Mrs. David Sayre, Price Cross, and Mrs. H.T. Beaver registered Aby kittens.

Price Cross of Texas imported Taishun Abigail that had been bred by E. Menezes. This female had been born on August 9, 1950. Ms. Menezes, incidentally, continues to be a devoted

An outstanding representative of the breed and the sire of many champions and grand champions is Gr. Ch. Chota-Li R.S.T. His influence on the Abyssinian breed can still be seen today. Breeder/owner: Edna Field.

breeder of Abyssinians to this day. She is active in the British fancy and is a GCCF (Governing Council of the Cat Fancy) judge. At about the same time, Mr. Cross imported a male cat named Raby Romeo, born on April 10, 1950, and bred by Lady Barnard.

Judy Smith now acquired cats from the Nigella Cattery and imported Nigella Mischa. The cat had been bred by Ms. Bone, and had been born on September 4, 1950. Before he was imported to the United States, Mischa had sired Taishun Josie, a female that had been born on August 8, 1951. Josie was imported by Mrs. Howard Stackhouse of New Jersey.

In 1952, for the first time, no Fairchild cats were registered in CFA stud books. Ms. Menezes sent Nepeta Wendy Girl to Ann Sayre. The dam of the cat was Taishun Pixie, and the sire was Merkland Negus. Another female Abyssinian cat was imported by Mr. and Mrs. James McCrae of Texas. Again, Ms. Menezes was the breeder and the cat was Taishun Dawn of Benmost Bore. The dam of the cat was Taishun Jasmin, and the sire was Nigella Mischa.

The number of Ms. Menezes' cats continued to increase in the United States. In 1952, Mrs. Waldo Schultz imported Taishun Zeta of Harmonie Acre. This cat had been born on April 27, 1952. Raby Chuffa, one of the most famous of all imports, was acquired by Frances Schuler Taft. The cat had been born on April 5, 1952, and had been bred by Lady Barnard. In 1953, Nigella Honey, bred by Ms. Bone, was imported by Mrs. Terry Vickers of California. The kitten had been born June 2, 1953.

Mrs. Lucas Combs of Kentucky imported a male named Abu of Knott Hall of Blue Grass. The kitten had been born April 20, 1953, and had been bred by Felix Tomilson. The sire was Albyn Jason, and the dam was Raby Ripple.

From 1954 through 1959 there was an ever-increasing group of Abyssinian breeders that included Virginia Daly, Lillian Magner, Mrs. C.W. Dixon, Mrs. Sol Talasnik, Mrs. William Fix, Harriet Wolfgang, Ruth Livingston, and Ruth McNaughton.

A most significant year in Abyssinian history was 1955, when Edna Field acquired her first Abyssinian. She then imported a pair from England named Chatwyn Taha and Deckham Penanon. Mrs. Field, who continued to breed Abyssinian cats and is a popular judge in CFA today, has contributed as much to the history of the breed in North America as anyone else. One interesting sidelight is that one of Mrs. Field's kittens went to Sheila Burnford, author of *The Incredible Journey*. The Aby kitten was a companion to old Simon, the Siamese cat in that story. Mrs. Field acquired stock from Christine Streetman and Harriet Zimmerman as well as from sources abroad, including German import Heidi of Chota-Li from John Koch. Some of Mrs. Field's well-known cats are Grand Champion Chota-Li R.S.T., Grand Champion Chota-Li Russet,

A fine head study of Dbl. Gr. and Quad. Ch. Selene's Firefly, a male, born May 22, 1957. Breeder: Francis Taft.

Opposite:
Fanciers who are serious about showing their cats enter as many cat shows as possible to see how their stock measures up to the competition. This Aby, who hasn't quite gotten over the shock of winning, may not realize what an honor it is to have just won a CFA Best Cat in Show award!

Grand Champion Chota-Li Flair, Grand Champion Chota-Li Fiesta of Fongin, Grand Champion Chota-Li Kahina of Phaulkon, and Grand Champion Chota-Li Mia. Russet was CFA Second Best Shorthair Female and Best Abyssinian in 1967-1968. In 1968-1969, Flair accomplished the same wins.

During the ensuing years, kittens were registered by Robin Brodie, Albert Hamling, Natalie Pyle, and Dorothy and Ernest Otten. In addition, Florence Kanoffe, Christine Streetman, Mrs. J.R. Ring, Neil Guild, and M. Harmer contributed to the Abyssinian breed in the United States. Louise Sample, past president of CFA, also bred many fine Abyssinians. Imports continued. Perhaps the most significant of these to the fancy was Rufus the Red of Selene, born on April 1, 1955. He was sired by Raby Chuffa of Selene and bred by Bonita Grauer from the dam Selene's Lise. Frances Schuler Taft acquired the cat.

Martha Prescott imported Deckham Abydos and Tranby Hequet. The cat Blackthorn Prunellia went to Mrs. David Sayre, while Blackthorn Sweet Sauterne was imported by Harry Charles.

The Djer-Mer Cattery had been transferred to Charles Johnson of Philadelphia, and during these significant years Mary Hantzmon registered kittens under her cattery name Merricourt. Elinor Dennis acquired Merricourt stock, and Christine Streetman of Texas had started with Selene stock from the Brodies. Maxine and Sherman Arps registered kittens in 1957. A well-known name in the cat fancy, Marjorie Pallady, acquired Bubu BaBa from the imported stock of Martha Prescott. Frances Herms had imported Heatherpine Rosetta. Mr. and Mrs. Manfield of Kansas imported Ronnvikens Nefertitie, a female, that had been born March 8, 1957. She had been bred from the Nigella stock by Fru M. Holmstrom. Nigella Fern, in turn, had been sired by a famous male, Nigella Contenti.

The January, 1959 issue of *Cat World* Magazine devoted itself to the Abyssinian breed. The cover of the magazine featured Grace Forrest's Grand Champion Bograe's Seb. Throughout the issue are photographs of some extraordinary Abyssinians; specifically, Calspuss Delire, Caper Cat Isis of Calspuss (belonging to Caroline Herz), and Grand Champion Abigail of Shermax. The issue of that magazine indicated the great popularity of the Abyssinian breed at that time.

In the late 1950's and early 1960's, Harriet Zimmerman, Erolyn Snelling, Aida Zanetti, and Dr. and Mrs. C. Wohlrabe became active Abyssinian breeders. Glenn Robberson and Len White imported Ronnvikens Tutankhamon, a male that had been born May 8, 1969, and had been bred by Fru Holmstrom.

The booklet *Journey From the Blue Nile,* produced by Aida Zanetti, Mary Hantzmon, and Elinor Dennis, became an addition to the very scarce writings about Abyssinians; there had been only one other pamphlet previously published by Mr. and Mrs. Denham in 1951, and it was entitled *Child of the Gods.*

Some significant cats were produced by Lynne VanderPoel when she obtained Selene and Samdur stock. Ms. VanderPoel bred Van Lyn's Tangelo, Van Lyn's Gold Bug, and Van Lyn's Gold Fleece of Van Dyke.

Harriet Cole Zimmerman obtained Sheramain's T. Twinks and Selene's Tammy; she also acquired Gold Bug from Ms. VanderPoel. A well-known cat, Aberdeen's Fire Ball, was born in February, 1964. The cat was bred by Harriet Zimmerman out of Tammy by T. Twinks. The litter brother of T. Twinks went from Mrs. McNaughtan to Charles and Alma Cowell. This cat was named Sheramain Yankee Sultan.

A particularly important year in Abyssinian history was 1963. During that year Grand Champion Pharoh Rameses II was bred by Carl and Kim Woodall (later Kim Everett). The cat's sire was Phil-Lori's Ki-O Kizan of Pharoh, and his dam was Ring's Aby Tanjii of Pharoh. During his show career Rameses II was the Second All-American Cat of the Year in 1965; he was Number One All-American Cat of the Year in 1966; in 1967 he was the Third All-American Cat of the Year. In 1966, he was also the Number Two CFA All-Star Cat and Best Shorthair. Rameses II is in the pedigrees of many fine Abyssinians being shown today. He was the sire of Holiday Hill Canile. This female, the dam of Holiday Hill Man O'War of Pharoh Loho, was bred by Joe McElroy. Man O'War was the sire of Pharoh Citation of Swingate. During 1972-1973, Citation was CFA's Best Cat. Another extraordinary Abyssinian of that time was Temas Pride of Pharoh, a female bred by Mr. and Mrs. Ted Stegent of Texas. This cat was acquired by Kim Everett. The sire of Temas Pride was Rameses II, and the dam was from Marjorie Pallady's stock, specifically Pallady's Bast of Temas.

Erolyn Snelling of Georgia contributed significantly to the Abyssinian breed when she began by acquiring Egypt of Es-Ta, bred by Mrs. T.A. Dobyns. She obtained from her friend Harriet Zimmerman a cat named Aberdeen's Tweed of Blue-Iris. Tweed was sired by T. Twinks and his dam was Gold Bug. Later, Erolyn Snelling imported Kobold of Blue-Iris from Mr. John Koch of Germany.

Dr. and Mrs. C. Wohlrabe, having bred excellent Abyssinians for several years, imported the litter brother of Kobold from Mr. Koch. The cat was Abou of Wohlrabe. A familiar name appears here because Frances Schuler Taft's cat, Selene's Jett, was the sire of Kobold and Abou. Abou sired many grand champions before his death in 1970.

Michael Goldfarb acquired Wohl-Rabe's Aahmes for his Mirkwood Cattery. He produced two extraordinary cats in Mirkwood Crispin, who was the sire of Mirkwood Gaston. The cat Tira, bred by Dr. and Mrs. Wohlrabe, went to Frank Roderick.

Beverly Risch acquired Wohl-Rabe's Shari. This cat was bred to Phil-Lori's Ki-O Kizan of Pharoh and produced Cairo's Katie of Holiday Hill. This grand champion was acquired by

Gr. Ch. Pharoh Citation of Swingate pictured with his breeder/owner, Bob Everett, at a 1972 Long Beach, California show. "Ci" was CFA's distinguished Best Cat for 1973. Breeders/owners: **Bob and Kim Everett.**

Opposite:
Gr. Ch. El Qahira's Chocolet . Breeder/owner:
Rae Ann Christ.

21

Ron and Judy Bauer. Katie has been the dam of two grand champions, Gallantree's Casey Jones and Gallantree's Davey Jones.

The litter brother of Katie went to Elizabeth Freret and at his maturity was Cairo's Kizan of Amulet. Ms. Freret, who had a short but active and intense career in breeding Abyssinians, had acquired stock from the late Mary Hantzmon and Dorothy Dimmock. The cats were Merricourt Ras Gabriel and Merricourt Debra. One of Elizabeth Freret's great cats was Amulet's Pepi, a cat that won many honors both as a kitten and an adult. Pepi was Best Kitten and also Second Best Cat in 1970. Upon the death of Mrs. Freret, Pepi went to Joan and Alfred Wastlhuber of California, and as Amulet's Pepi of Nepenthes, provided the foundation for their future breedings.

Thelma Walner of Texas acquired Abyssinians from Christine Streetman and Frances Schuler Taft to start her Chac-Ma Cattery.

Misty Mornin' Mango, bred by Charles Milwain, went to Donna Jean Thompson. Ms. Thompson bred Mango to Edna Field's Chota-Li R.S.T. and produced Jeannel Charlie. Charlie was the Best Abyssinian Cat in 1971 and the sire of many grand champions. The cat Mango had been bred by Mr. Milwain from Erolyn Snelling's stock. The sire of Mango was Kobold of Blue-Iris, and the dam was Blue-Iris Tru So of Misty Mornin'. Jeannel Charlie sired Jeannel B.C. and Gallantree's Davey Jones; both of these cats became grand champions.

Blue-Iris stock went to Hertha Farmer (later Chellevold) from Erolyn Snelling. The cat was Blue-Iris Tuk Tweed. Additionally, Mrs. Farmer acquired Wohl-Rabe's Tara Rameses from the Wohlrabes to begin the Avenue Cattery.

The circle of Abyssinian breeders grew larger; some produced excellent stock that provided future grand champions in the exhibition rings. Others produced one or two grand champions and did little else for the heritage of the breed.

In 1970, Cairo's Katie of Holiday Hill, Mar-Jon's FireFly, Mirkwood Crispin, and Quin-Jo's Katari achieved grand champion status.

The 1971 season found three grand champions that had been sired by Chota-Li R.S.T. They were Chota-Li Kahina of Phaulkon, owned by the Mahers; Chota-Li Sienna of Quin-Jo, owned by Rich and Becky Jones; and Jeannel Charlie, Best Aby of the Year. Among the other fine cats of that year were Mirkwood Gaston of Abyiat, bred by the Goldfarbs and owned by Brenda Garnett, and the Wohlrabes' Wohl-Rabe's Zakari of Hi-Ab and Wohl-Rabe's Hadji-Baba of Ma-Jah.

In 1972 some spectacular Abyssinians were shown. Amulet's Ankha of Ja Bob, bred by Elizabeth Freret, Chota-Li Cricket of Phaulkon, and three Etta-Mert Abys were made grand champions. Mirkwood Gaston of Abyiat was Fourth Best Cat in the national standings.

Gr. Ch. Anshent-won's Makeba of Soketumi. Breeders: Dr. and Mrs. John W. Boyd (Joyce Chang). Owners: Carlton Smith and Rita Rerat.

In 1972-1973, Pharoh Citation of Swingate was the Best Cat in the United States. His remarkable show record included 124 Best of Breed wins and 90 Best in Show awards. During the same season, El Qahira's Deseret, bred by Rae Ann Christ, was among the grand champions.

The 1973-1974 show season included more Aby grands. Quin-Jo's Brass Tacks, bred by Rich and Becky Jones, was shown to grand championship. Ron and Judy Bauer produced three grand champions, Gallantree's Hobie Cat, Lancer, and Kristy. (A significant event was the death of that great cat Amulet's Pepi of Nepenthes.)

CFA's Best Aby was Grand Champion Queen Tiye's Renaissance of O-Wen, bred by Jean Soper and owned by Carolyn Owen. Later she was the dam of Grand Champion O-Wen's Macho and Grand Champion O-Wen's Latigo. Her littermate was Grand Champion Queen Tiye's Jessica. Jean Soper also produced other excellent Abys, among which were Grand Champion Queen Tiye's Kaiffossus of Ursis, owned by Marge Orsini; Grand Champion Queen Tiye's Joel, and Grand Champion Queen Tiye's Demet, both owned by Pat Brauel.

The Best Abyssinian in 1974-1975 was Colbyshire Cochise of Quin-Jo, bred by Bob and Kitty Colby and owned by Rich and Becky Jones. Among the grand champions were Anshent-Won's Anasazi and Anshent-Won's Makeba, bred by John and Joyce (Chang) Boyd. A particularly outstanding Abyssinian of that year was Bastis Zackariah, bred and owned by Robert Chorneau and Wain Harding. Companion Cat Neb En Sebau was the best Red Aby, and the breeder was Pamela Black. Etta-Mert Town Talk of Phaulkon, bred by Mr. and Mrs. Merton Landon and owned by Sylvia Fitzgerald, also achieved grand champion status.

In 1975 and 1976, Rae Ann Christ's cat El Qahira's Sharm El was Seventh Best Cat, while Avenue Pepi-Tbasko of Nepenthes was the Tenth Best Cat. Pepi-Tbasko was bred by Duane and Hertha Chellevold and owned by the Wastlhubers. His sire was Amulet's Pepi of Nepenthes, and his grand sire was Cairo Kizan of Amulet, CFA's Best Shorthair Male in 1969. (A most significant event was the death of Chota-Li R.S.T. This cat was one of the greatest sires of all time. He was born in March, 1966, and died in November, 1975.) Among the grand champions of that season were Anshent-Won's Maya of Gallantree, Bastis Face to Face, and Bastis Glitters N'Glows. The Cyan Cattery produced two important cats, Cyan's R.P.L. and Cyan's Kodachrome of Helium. Rae Ann Christ's cat El Qahira's Hot Toddy started his climb to fame. The Landons produced five grand champions that year. They were Etta-Mert Mitchell, Etta-Mert Foreglow, Etta-Mert Tamarack, Etta-Mert Trader, and Etta-Mert Trademark of Orca.

Best Aby of 1976-1977 was Los Colorado's Amiga, bred by Marilyn Fuentes. A remarkable group of Abyssinians bred by

Gr. Ch. Jeannel Charlie, son of Gr. Ch. Chota-Li R.S.T., is himself
sire of many grand champions and was CFA's Best Abyssinian,
1971. Breeder/owner: Donna Jean Thompson.

Opposite:
Gr. Ch. El Qahira's Deseret in a noble stance
similar to that of the cats portrayed in ancient
Egyptian art. Breeder/owner: Rae Ann Christ.

Gr. Ch. O-Wen's Latigo (left) and Gr. Ch. O-Wen's Macho (right) are both grandsons of Gr. Ch. Pharoh Citation of Swingate. By Gr. Ch. Pallady's Native Dancer x Gr. Ch. Queen Tiye's Renaissance of O-Wen. Breeders/owners: Kerry and Carolyn Owen.

the Boyds became grand champions, and they included: Anshent-Won Anahita, Anshent-Won Margaux, Anshent-Won's Manani, Anshent-Won's Mesabi, and Anshent-Won Ariba. Manani and Ariba went to the Soketumi Cattery, owned by Carlton Smith and Rita Rerat. Among the other grand champions of that year were: Morningside Buzz, bred and owned by Ernest and Dorothy Otten, who were among the earliest breeders of Abyssinians in the United States; Nepenthes Tquilla of Badfinger; Nepenthes Leo; O-Wen's Latigo; O-Wen's Macho; Quin-Jo's Butternut of Sunnerise; and Queen Tiye's Joel.

The 1977-1978 show season included two Abyssinians in the Top Twenty CFA cats. Anshent-Won's Manani of Soketumi was Eleventh Best Cat and Bastis Panama Red, bred by Wain Harding, was Nineteenth Best Cat. The Second Best Shorthair Kitten, one which would achieve great success the following year, was Soketumi Samadari, bred and owned by Carlton Smith and Rita Rerat.

Two litter brothers granded that year, Sunnerise Beechnut and Sunnerise Laburnum of Erinwood. Also achieving grand champion status were two outstanding red littermates, Badfinger's Bumble Bee and Badfinger's Genesis, sired by Zackariah. (Another littermate granded in 1979, Badfinger's Kalua of Avelion.) Badfinger Cattery, owned by Laura Thompson, has produced many outstanding cats, including Badfinger's Bumin' Around T.Q., Badfinger's Kandy Kiss of Gemtone, Badfinger's Lyon of Darken, and Badfinger's Pinata.

Nepenthes Cattery, owned by Alfred and Joan Wastlhuber, produced two spectacular litters that year with several cats achieving grand champion status. These were Nepenthes Dubonnet, Nepenthes Khari of Shagrat, Nepenthes Peprika, and Nepenthes Prophet of Dar-Ling. DuBonnet and Prophet are litter brothers of Grand Champion Nepenthes Leo and Grand Champion Nepenthes Tquilla of Badfinger. Khari and Peprika were sired by Leo.

The 1978-1979 season showed Soketumi Samadari and Nepenthes Nereus among the top winners of CFA cats. Samadari achieved Third Best Cat and Nereus, Fourth Best Cat. In addition, Quin-Jo's Cardinal, bred and owned by Rich and Becky Jones, was Ninth Best Cat. This male was sired by Grand Champion Bastis Zackariah. This was truly an outstanding year for Abys.

In 1979-1980, CFA's Top Abyssinian was Grand Champion Nepenthes Akime. The Best Shorthair Kitten and Second Best CFA Kitten was Grand Champion Nepenthes Esprit.

In the 1980-1981 show season, Grand Champion Cinna's Jack Daniels granded in one show and then went on to become CFA's Best Abyssinian and Tenth Best Cat. Two beautiful Abyssinians were shown that year: Grand Champion Lakme Kalahari of Raelich and Grand Champion Abydos Phoenix, son of Soketumi Samadari.

The history of the Abyssinian breed has been relatively short compared to that of some other breeds, but the quality of the cats has not been surpassed. Future Abyssinian breeders have a great heritage upon which to build.

Above: Gr. Ch. Nepenthes Leo. Breeders/owners: Joan and Alfred Wastlhuber. Below: Gr. Ch. Nepenthes Khari of Shagrat (sired by Leo, above). Breeders: Joan and Alfred Wastlhuber. Owner: Candice Wilson.

Gr. Ch. Bastis Zacka-
riah, D.M. (right). Breed-
ers/owners: Wain Hard-
ing and Bob Chorneau.
D.M. stands for Distin-
guished Merit, a title
awarded to top produc-
ing male and female
cats. Gr. Ch. Nepenthes
Peprika (another of
Leo's offspring) pictured
at 10 weeks (below).
Breeders: Joan and
Alfred Wastlhuber.
Owners: Tom and Sheila
Leaman.

EARLY BRITISH ABYSSINIANS

Date of Birth	Cat	Sire	Dam	Breeder
1892	Sedgemere Bottle	Unknown	Unknown	Swinyard
1894	Sedgemere Peaty	Unknown	Unknown	Swinyard
3/23/01	Princess Alice	Namsham	Alice	Pitkin
4/05/01	Pynt	Unknown	Kitty Link	Frederick
7/?/03	Fancy Free	Unknown	Unknown	Carew-Cox
7/13/05	Aluminum	Ras Kasir	Rocksham	Carew-Cox
9/19/05	Woggs	Unknown	Kitty Link	Frederick
1/22/06	Tsaha	Ras Kasir	Linga	Carew-Cox
3/02/06	Cojam	Unknown	Fancy Free	Carew-Cox
2/17/07	King Theodore	Ras Kasar	Fancy Free	Carew-Cox
6/30/07	Queen Olna	Unknown	Unknown	Roberts
7/17/07	Bunnie	Chipsie	Pynt	Frederick
7/20/07	Roguvald	Unknown	Unknown	Roberts (owner)
9/03/07	Quicksilver	Aluminum	Fancy Free	Carew-Cox
9/03/07	Aluminum II	Aluminum	Fancy Free	Carew-Cox
9/30/07	Beautiful II	Chipsie	Woggs	Frederick
10/12/07	Silver Memelik	Unknown	Fulmer Flossie	Lady Decies
10/23/07	Pepper	Aluminum	Abeba	Carew-Cox
10/23/07	Salt	Aluminum	Abeba	Carew-Cox
1/27/08	Tsana of Bath	Ras Kamar	Linga	Carew-Cox
3/02/08	Silver Fairy	Aluminum	Fancy Free	Carew-Cox
3/02/08	Platinum of Thorpe	Aluminum	Fancy Free	Carew-Cox
4/25/08	Ras Dashan	Aluminum	Linga	Carew-Cox
4/25/08	Poddie	Chipsie	Woggs	Frederick
5/14/08	Thebau	Dervish	Quicksilver	Lady Douglas-Pennant
Unknown	Dervism	Unknown	Unknown	Baskett
3/12/09	African Queen of Ravenor	Ras Dashan	Lady Mantana	Patman
3/24/10	Antalo	Ras Dashan	Lady Mantana	Patman
3/24/10	Queen Baucis of Peter Head	Ras Dashan	Lady Mantana	Patman
4/10/09	Dickon	Beautiful II	Mysouf	Frederick
7/20/10	Weybourne Joshua	Ras Dashan	Lady Mantana	Patman
3/23/11	Tessama	Quizero Taitou	Alcara	Woodman
6/03/11	Adis Ababa	Ras Dashan	Silver Ideal	Clarke
7/03/11	Oxney Dot	Oxney Pride	Queenie	Pitkin
4/07/12	Puma	Quizero Taitou	Queen Baucis	Carew-Cox
4/07/12	Caracul	Quizero Taitou	Queen Baucis	Carew-Cox
7/11/12	Adna	Ras Dashan	Tessama	Woodman
7/11/12	Bonca	Ras Dashan	Tessama	Woodman

NOTABLE IMPORTS FROM GREAT BRITAIN TO THE UNITED STATES

Date of Birth	Cat	Sire	Dam	Breeder	Importer
9/07/07	Aluminum II	Aluminum	Fancy Free	Carew-Cox	Cathcart
10/25/07	Salt	Aluminum	Abeba	Carew-Cox	Cathcart
12/?/33	Woodroofe Ena of Newton	Woodroofe Danus	Woodroofe Aura	Woodiwiss	Cobb
4/03/38	Djer-Mer's Croham Isana	Croham Menelik	Woodroofe Justa	C. Basnett	Djer-Mer
4/03/38	Djer-Mer's Croham Justina	Croham Menelik	Woodroofe Justa	C. Basnett	Djer-Mer
5/21/48	Raby Aida	Raby Ashanto	Wagphur Cleopatra	Lady Barnard	B. Warren
5/21/48	Raby Nefertari	Raby Ashanto	Wagphur Cleopatra	Lady Barnard	B. Warren
5/21/48	Raby Ramphis	Raby Ashanto	Wagphur Cleopatra	Lady Barnard	Kloos
5/29/48	Merkland Sheba	Kreeoro Kaffa	Merkland Telari	Liverpool	Kloos
3/26/49	Merkland Magdala	Kreeoro Kaffa	Merkland Telari	Liverpool	B. Warren
3/26/49	Merkland Habesh	Kreeoro Kaffa	Merkland Telari	Liverpool	B. Warren
5/21/49	Pussner Paragon	Kreeoro Kaffa	Straw	Hedlam	Smith
6/18/49	Pussner Pride	Raby Ashanto	Pussner Cat	Hedlam	Smith
8/07/49	Merkland Dembea	Croham Abeba	Merkland Telari	Liverpool	Hoeller
8/07/49	Merkland Takazza	Croham Abeba	Merkland Telari	Liverpool	Hoeller
4/09/50	Nigella Mimi	Croham Abeba	Merkland Adowa	Bone	Porter
4/10/50	Raby Romeo	Raby Ashanto	Raby Tosca	Barnard	Cross
4/27/50	Croham Zena	Croham Abeba	Croham Gondar	C. Basnett	Porter
8/09/50	Taishun Abigail	Merkland Negus	Taishun Pixie	Menezes	Cross
9/04/50	Nigella Mischa	Croham Abeba	Merkland Adowa	Bone	Smith
4/04/51	Nepeta Wendy Girl	Merkland Negus	Taishun Pixie	Menezes	Sayre
5/21/51	Taishun Dawn	Nigella Mischa	Taishun Jasmin	Menezes	McCrae
8/08/51	Taishun Josie	Nigella Mischa	Taishun Mehalek	Menezes	Stackhouse
4/05/52	Raby Chuffa	Raby Ashanto	Raby Tosca	Barnard	Schuler
4/27/52	Taishun Zeta	Croham Abeba	Taishun Sadie	Menezes	Schultz
4/20/53	Abu of Knott Hall	Albyn Jason	Raby Ripple	Tomilson	Combs
6/02/53	Nigella Honey	Bruene Achilles	Heatherpine Juanita	Bone	Vickers
5/07/56	Chatwyn Taha	Bruene Achilles	Blackthorn Marsala	Tancock	Field
8/15/56	Deckham Penanon	Heatherpine Nimrod	Deckham Deliah	Stuart	Field
4/13/57	Deckham Abydos	Nigella Rashid	Deckham Deliah	Stuart	Prescott
6/01/57	Tranby Hequet	Merkland Negus	Tranby Lotos	Windsor	Prescott

Many theorists believe that the Abyssinian breed, as we know it today, developed as a result of selective breeding efforts by feline enthusiasts in England. British Domestic Shorthairs, together with imported cats, were the foundation for their breeding programs, and through years of experimentation, breeders were able to perfect the Aby type that they were so desperately trying to achieve. Above and left are charts which outline the early history of the breed from Britain to the United States. Charts reprinted with permission from the Cat Fanciers' Association, Inc.

The CFA Abyssinian standard calls for eyes that are "almond-shaped, large, brilliant, and expressive. Neither round nor Oriental. Eyes accentuated by dark lidskin, encircled by light-colored area."

Opposite:
Even at the tender age of five weeks, these adorable females (above) display the characteristic Aby facial markings. Breeders/owners: Joan and Alfred Wastlhuber. Ten-week-old Nepenthes Diablo of Valley and his littermate (below) have started to grow their thick adult coats. Breeders: Joan and Alfred Wastlhuber. Owner: Penny Maxwell.

Abyssinian kittens are a joy to own, but before making your final decision to purchase one, be certain that you can take full responsibility for this little creature's well being. Abys are extremely affectionate and intelligent and will need lots of love and attention. They will also need plenty of space for exercise and play; a complete, nutritionally balanced diet; a warm, cozy place to sleep; and good medical care.

34

Your New Abyssinian

Where to Find an Abyssinian

Abys can be located through veterinary clinics, national cat magazines, or by attending cat shows. It is wise to familiarize yourself with the major pedigree lines in your area. If possible, try to observe and evaluate as many Abys as you can before you make a decision. Attending a cat show will allow you to meet several breeders at one time, observe winning cats, and talk to knowledgeable people about all aspects of cat ownership.

Buying from a breeder will allow you to see the parents or other relatives of the kitten. In addition, most breeders are willing to supply help and information, should you ever need it in the future.

When visiting a cattery, be sure to examine the kittens' home environment. Make sure the facilities are clean. Many breeders will cage young kittens for their own protection; however, the kittens should be let out frequently for exercise and socialization to the normal home life. This will let them develop the kind of manners and attitudes needed to make good pets.

The Right Age for a New Home

Seldom is a kitten seen that is more adorable than the Abyssinian. The tabby markings around the face and the large ears give a delightfully mischievous expression.

Abyssinians mature more slowly than other breeds. Males sometimes do not reach total adulthood until one and one-half to two years. An eight-week-old kitten might appear to be six weeks old to a person not familiar with the breed. For those who wish a cat would stay a kitten just a little bit longer, this is a distinct advantage.

When Aby kittens are born, they have a downy coat. They are not ticked, although the stripe down the back and the facial markings are present. The baby fur is gradually exchanged for the adult hair starting at about six weeks of age. During this transition, the soft, short kitten fur is patched and interspaced with the longer, thicker adult hair.

The color of the eyes when first opened is a gray-blue. This gradually turns a muddy brown which fades into green or gold. Either color is acceptable for showing, but most people prefer the rich gold color.

Kittens are rarely sold by reputable breeders before they are fully weaned. By about 12 weeks, a kitten is usually eating solid food, is litter box trained, and is ready to adjust to a new environment. These littermates (left and below) seek each other's companionship and security. The Aby (opposite), like most cats, must satisfy its curiosity by exploring and examining everything within its reach. Here this fellow enjoys being part of the holiday pageantry.

The best age to acquire your cat is between 12 and 16 weeks. By this time most of the adult hair has developed, and the kitten has matured to just the right size.

Abys are excellent mothers, and their kittens form very strong attachments to them. However, at about 12 weeks the kittens begin to transfer this affection to the people around them. It will be easier if the attachment is made to the new owner and not the breeder. Also, about this age an Aby's intense curiosity will allow it to adjust to a new environment with excitement and interest instead of hesitation.

Classes of Kittens

Most breeders will evaluate all of the kittens in a litter and, based on experience, will place them in one of three basic groups. The largest group will be the pet kittens. These Abys do not meet the standard for the breed in some way. This could be a disqualifying fault, such as a white spot (locket) on the throat or extensive gray roots of the hair. It may be something less serious—for example, a roundish head or barring on the legs. Also included as pets are older cats that are no longer needed for breeding. Often it takes an experienced eye to detect the reason the kitten has been placed in this category. Pet Abys are in no way less beautiful or less healthy cats; however, they are not quite what the breeder would like them to be in terms of the standard of perfection.

Reputable breeders will insist on a "neuter-spay agreement" when selling their pet Abys. This is a contract which states that owners agree to have their kittens altered at an appropriate age. Registration papers and pedigree may be withheld by the breeder until the owner has sent a veterinarian's certificate confirming the altering. This insures that only the best kittens are allowed to continue the breed. By following this agreement, you are ensuring that the Abyssinian breed will continue to improve.

In the second class of kittens are the breeding quality cats. These Abys match the standard closely enough to be used to improve the breed. Such kittens are often kept until they are almost adults before the breeder makes a final decision as to how they might best be used.

In the last class of kittens are show cats. These rare kittens are what every good breeder strives for. They match the standard so closely that they can compete with the many beautiful Abyssinians currently being shown at cat shows.

Male or Female?

Once your kitten is altered, the original sex is of little consequence. Unaltered cats of *any* breed simply do not make good pets. Both the males and females can spray urine to advertise and mark their territories. Tomcat urine, in particular, has a very unpleasant and penetrating odor. In addition, the sex drive is so strong that the cat is preoccupied much of the time with trying to satisfy it. This leaves little of its attention for you and your family.

This four-week-old male, Sunbeau, is still too young to leave his mother. He needs more time to grow and to develop the kind of social behavior that is desirable in a good pet. By Ch. Pharaoh of Badfinger x Ch. Helium's Starfire. Breeder/owner: Jeanclaire Bridgers.

Breeders of purebred cats usually evaluate a litter by classifying each individual kitten according to how well it fits the standard (an esthetic ideal established by an official cat registering organization) for the breed. Generally, kittens fall into one of three classes: pet, breeder, or show.

The spaying operation (ovariohysterectomy) for females involves the removal of the uterus and ovaries. The surgery is done under anesthesia, so no pain is felt by the cat. In most cases, your Aby is ready to return home the next day with only a tiny incision visible. Approximately eight to ten months is the ideal age for this operation to be performed, as most growth has occurred by then.

The neutering or castration surgery for males is a simpler procedure because it does not involve entering the cat's abdominal cavity. The testicles are removed, and the scrotum generally is not sutured.

Both operations are very routine and safe. Your Aby will not be aware that a change has taken place because the influence of the hormones wears off gradually. The cat is not a human being so it does not view the removal of sex organs as a person would. The net result will be a happier, healthier pet without the all-consuming sex drive.

After the surgery, your pet may require fewer calories in its diet. If it begins to gain weight, simply reduce the amount of food you feed. Most Abys, however, do not have a problem with their weight.

Some owners are concerned about a possible personality change after surgery. Should this occur, it will be a positive one toward becoming a more loving member of the family.

More important than sex when selecting a kitten is the individual personality, which is not dependent on gender. If you plan to begin breeding and showing, a female is by far the better choice. When you have obtained several females and have gained some experience, then purchasing a male is worthwhile. Something else to consider when making your purchase is that male Abys do develop heavier bone structure than the females, which tend to be daintier.

Gr. Ch. Bromide Kye-En of Sirkarah, a red Abyssinian. Breeders: Kate and Karl Faler. Owner: Jane Carpenter. This show-quality Aby has what it takes to compete in the show ring with other top caliber members of the breed.

Above: Avenue Starr of Nepenthes. Breeders: Duane and Hertha Chellevold. Owners: Joan and Alfred Wastlhuber. **Right:** Gr. Ch. Nepenthes Leo. Breeders/owners: Joan and Alfred Wastlhuber. Abys that are allowed out-of-doors should always be supervised in an enclosed area.

Indoors or Outdoors?

There is a myth that Abyssinians do not adjust to an indoor life. It is true that they need daily attention and exercise to be healthy, but this can easily be provided indoors. In fact, almost all breeders insist that their kittens be let out only in an enclosed run or on a leash. A cat allowed to roam freely encounters danger every day in the form of dogs, cars, poisons, etc. No amount of training can teach a cat to stay away from these hazards 100% of the time. Breeders have put much time and effort into raising healthy kittens and want them to live a long and happy life. If you care about your kitten, you will want the best for it. This involves protection from things it does not understand and cannot avoid.

Choosing a Kitten

If you plan to purchase an Aby kitten from a breeder, you may have to visit the cattery several times in order to judge the kitten's personality. Watch the kitten at play; find out whether it is aggressive, shy, inactive, and so forth. Observe how it interacts with the breeder and with its littermates. The breeder should be able to give you an objective evaluation of the kitten's strong and weak qualities. It is best to keep in mind that much of the molding of the personality will take place after the kitten is established in its new home. However, a sour disposition *can* be inherited from one or both of its parents. Like a child, whose early experiences may set later behavior patterns,

If your source for buying an Abyssinian kitten is a breeder, chances are you may be able to see and to evaluate an entire litter and one or both of its parents.

it is important that a kitten be raised in a happy and loving home environment.

Examine the kitten for good health. Check to see there is no foreign matter around the eyes, ears, and nose. Runny eyes and nose could be a sign of upper respiratory infection, and black granular material in the ears could indicate ear mites. The hair coat should be shiny, with a spring to it; this indicates a good diet and reflects overall health. Most breeders will not object if you wish to have your veterinarian check the kitten. No matter how enticing a kitten is, if it is not healthy and strong, it is not the one to choose. Remember, the kitten will be a member of your family for years to come, so take time in your selection.

What You Should Know About Your Kitten

The kitten you purchase should have received a full series of vaccinations against both upper respiratory diseases and feline panleukopenia (distemper) by the time it is ready for a new home. Some breeders will supply a certificate that the Aby has tested negative for Leukemia.

Question the person from whom you purchased your Abyssinian about the kitten's usual diet. A rapid change of food is stressful to a young Aby. It is best to change over to a new diet by mixing some new food with some of the accustomed food. Gradually increase the amount of new food until the switch has been made. Even a rapid change of water can be upsetting to some Abyssinians. Watch the kitten carefully to make sure it has located its new dining area and the excitement has not caused it to forget to eat.

Opposite above: Ch. Bromide Indium in a thoughtful pose. Breeders/owners: Kate and Karl Faler. **Opposite below:** Show cats should learn at an early age to become accustomed to being confined for both short and long periods in a show cage. **Right:** Gr. Ch. Nepenthes Narcissa II of Spartacus pictured at four months. Breeders: Joan and Alfred Wastlhuber. Owners: Ruth Bauer and Lissa Fried. **Below:** Gr. Ch. Nepenthes Nereus, CFA's Fourth Best Cat, Best Shorthair, and Best Aby, 1979. Breeders/owners: Joan and Alfred Wastlhuber.

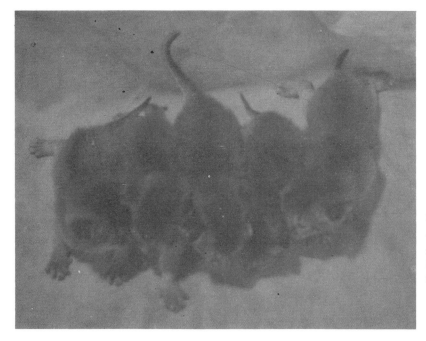

A two-week-old litter of ruddies. These young kits are not yet characterized by their ticked coats (ticking develops later on); however, they are born with a noticeable dark dorsal stripe.

Taking the Kitten Home

Your Aby kitten will most likely be apprehensive about going to its new home, so it is important to offer loving reassurance whenever possible so that it knows it is safe and in good hands. Buy or borrow a cat carrier in which to transport your new kitten home. If you are unable to borrow a carrier, there are inexpensive ones commercially available. The dark, closed-in feeling of a carrier will help make your kitten feel secure while riding in the car, especially if the kitten cannot see the passing scenery. (Cats have a very good sense of equilibrium and seldom suffer from motion sickness, but the sight of passing objects can be very upsetting to them.) The carrier will eliminate the need for the driver or other passengers in the car to fend off an hysterical cat; additionally, the confined kitten will not be able to escape through an open car door or window.

Many Abyssinians love to travel and will walk around in the car with nonchalance, but this behavior takes some time to develop. (I know of Abys that take hiking trips riding on their owners' backpacks, Abys that go sailing, and even those that enjoy a jaunt on a motorcycle!) Some cats adjust best over the course of a long trip; others require a gradual exposure by many short journeys; some may never adjust to traveling. In any case, whenever traveling, reassure your Aby by speaking calmly to it, and offer small tidbits of its favorite food if necessary.

When you arrive home with your new kitten, let it out of the carrier and into a small room to explore. Once the kitten is at home in this room, then it can be introduced to the rest of the house. If the kitten becomes insecure or frightened, it will have a familiar place to come back to. This method should prevent the typical problem of "a kitten who hides under the couch for the first few days in its new home" from occurring.

Opposite:
Kittens need time to adjust to new surroundings. Offer lots of love and reassurance as your Aby explores and becomes familiar with its new home.

Nature has equipped cats, both domestic and wild, with extraordinarily keen senses that are necessary for survival. Often kittens can be seen acting out their predatory instincts during play. Crouching low in a watchful position, chasing, pouncing, batting with the paws, are all part of normal kitten behavior.

Opposite:
Ch. Bromide Neptunium. Breeders/owners: Kate and Karl Faler.

The Litter Box

When you first bring your new Aby kitten home, the litter box (or pan) that you provide should contain the type of litter with which the kitten is familiar. This might be sand, gravel, wood shavings, pellets, or newspaper. If you wish to change to another type, wait until the kitten has settled into its new home; then gradually change the proportions from the former litter to the new until the adjustment is complete. The use of non-commercial litter, such as earth or sand, is *not* recommended due to the possibility of its contamination with microorganisms or parasites; additionally, some clay and vegetable matter litters will form hard lumps in the bottom of the litter box once they have absorbed moisture, so these, too, are not recommended. While newspaper is readily available and a relatively inexpensive litter material, it does not absorb moisture or odors very well. The most effective litter materials available today are commercially prepared ones. Many litters contain special additives that help control, and sometimes eliminate, litter box odors. There are also a variety of sprays and liquids designed to eliminate odors; check your local pet shop for those products that suit you and your Aby.

The best type of litter box to use is the commercially available large, rectangular variety. These are constructed so they will not absorb odors, and they are usually large enough to accommodate most cats so that they do not have to "perch" on the sides of the box. Some litter boxes are equipped with a top lip or with a complete cover with a door opening to eliminate the problem of scattered or spilled litter material, which often occurs when a cat buries its droppings deep in the litter.

It is doubtful whether a mother cat "trains" her kittens to use the litter box. A kitten's instinct to bury its wastes comes naturally, and this behavior can be easily channeled by providing the best material for this purpose. If a kitten is not provided with a suitable litter box and litter material, it may, unfortunately, choose its own location, such as the carpeting, your bedding, or perhaps on top of a pile of clothes. Good behavior can become a habit just as easily as bad behavior, so this is why the litter box should be located in a convenient spot where your Aby will pass by it many times during the day. A busy kitten may break training if it has to make a special effort to find its litter box in the basement or in other out-of-the-way places. For the first few days, place the kitten inside its litter box after meals and naps. (See "Adjusting to Other Pets and Children" section for how to lift and carry your Aby.) This is good insurance against mistakes. Most Abys, incidentally, learn to use the litter box when they first begin to eat solid food, long before they are weaned from their mother. If you purchase a kitten that is between the ages of 12 and 16 weeks (as suggested earlier), it should already be fully weaned *and* litter trained.

Abyssinians are exceptionally fastidious animals, and they may refuse to use their litter box unless it is kept scrupulously

By the time a kitten is completely weaned from its mother, it should be thoroughly familiar with toilet training and the litter box. Keeping the litter box clean and in a convenient spot is a sure way of eliciting good behavior from your pet. Litter pan liners facilitate the job of litter disposal.

clean; therefore, it is important to remove all solid wastes from the litter box daily. Litter material should be changed frequently, as needed. Occasionally, adult cats may break house training. Sexually active male and female cats use urine-marked places as a means of communication; however, altering usually will prevent this from occurring. Abys are very sensitive to family life, and they may express their displeasure, confusion, or unhappiness by not using their litter box (Volmer, 1979). Certain diseases, particularly FUS (feline urologic syndrome), can cause lack of control. It is best to determine the cause of any problem, as it will often suggest a remedy. If your Aby is eliminating in a consistent spot, you may have to use mothballs as a repellent, provide a second litter box, or move a piece of furniture onto the area in order to solve the problem. It is important to remove all traces of odor from the soiled area so the mistake does not keep recurring. On the other hand, if the cat is using several areas other than its litter box, a period of confinement with a clean, handy box may result in retraining. The best approach is prevention, which means *always* having a clean, convenient litter box available.

Scratching

All cats have a natural urge to use their claws. Scratching and clawing actions are normal and cause small peelings to be shed off the sides of the nail. This is instinctual, as in the natural state, and it leaves a visual territorial sign for other cats (Beaver, 1976). The net result is a sharper claw and often a less pleasant pet for the owner.

Clipping the claws is a *must* for your indoor Aby. Use a pair of claw clippers specifically designed for cats; most pet shops stock these. The first few times you attempt to clip the claws, you may need someone to help you hold the cat's feet. Try to make claw trimming as pleasant as possible by giving your Aby extra petting and praise before, during, and after the procedure.

As you begin, press the joint just behind the claw gently between your thumb and index finger. This will extend the claw. Note that there is a pink area which extends downward from the claw bed. Be careful not to cut into this region, as you may clip a nerve or blood vessel; this can be painful to your Aby and it can make the chore more difficult next time. Cut the claw with a quick motion to avoid excessive splintering. Clip both the front and back claws, and don't forget that the front feet have an extra claw on the inside of the leg called the "dew claw." Do not stop trimming if the cat struggles; otherwise, it is sure to try to slip away the next time. Abyssinians learn fast. Have someone assist you by holding the cat still. Claw trimming should be done approximately once a month to keep your Aby's claws in good condition.

Clipping the claws will reduce the amount of scratching, but it will not eliminate it entirely; therefore, a scratching post must be provided. There are a wide variety of scratching posts available, including those made of wood, carpeting, cardboard, or cork. There are many styles and sizes from which to choose. Whichever one you purchase can be made more attractive to your kitten by attaching a dangling toy (that is securely fastened) to it, or for an older cat, by spraying it with an aerosol catnip. (*Note:* Kittens tend to be repelled rather than attracted by the smell of catnip.) Try to select a scratching post that is long enough for your Aby to stretch out on.

As soon as you bring your new Aby home, introduce it to the scratching post. Whenever you see your kitten scratching in an inappropriate place, discourage it with a loud noise, a squirt of water, or with something else the cat dislikes. Then, immediately place your Aby on the scratching post and make scratching motions with its front paws. While doing this, offer praise for the action. If you are consistent with this training, your Aby soon will learn what you desire.

Declawing (onchyectomy) should be reserved as a last resort when claw trimming and training are not successful. This surgery (under anesthesia) involves removing the claws to the first joint. The operation should be performed when the kitten is as young as possible, although many older cats have been known

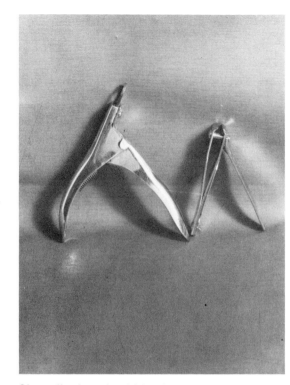

Claw clipping should begin when your Aby is young (about eight weeks) so that it becomes accustomed to the procedure. Claw clippers are available in most pet shops.

Restrain the cat securely and hold one paw. Be gentle but firm during the clipping process, while reassuring the cat with words of praise.

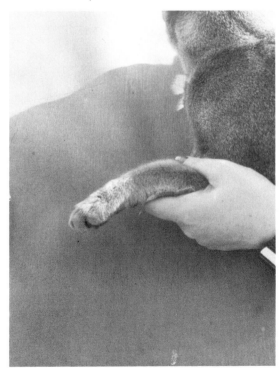

While holding the cat's paw, gently press on the joint just behind one of the claws. As the claw extends, note the pink area, or quick, at the base of the claw. Avoid cutting into this sensitive area.

While the claw is fully extended, clip it with a quick motion. Repeat this clipping procedure for each claw on all four paws.

to adjust quite well. When your Aby's feet heal, they will appear flatter than normal, and your cat or kitten will continue to make claw sharpening motions. Declawed cats are at a disadvantage and should *never* be let outdoors.

Even when the claws have been clipped or removed, some kittens can become too rough when playing. When kittens are young and play too hard with their littermates, their siblings communicate that they are being hurt by biting, hissing, or crying. You, too, must let your cat know when it is hurting you. A soft cuff, such as a mother cat gives her kittens when they misbehave, seems to work best. Do not encourage your Aby kitten to play with your hands; substitute a toy instead.

Adjusting to Other Pets and Children

The kitten will not have much of a problem adjusting to other cats. It has, after all, been raised with other felines (its litter mates) and has learned how to get along. However, if you already have a cat, some care in introducing the new family member must be exercised.

Cats are territorial by nature, perhaps as a natural adaptation on their part to keep their territories from being over-hunted. The natural reaction of a cat when meeting a stranger on its home property is to drive the intruder away. It is important, then, that the two cats are aware of each other but separated until they come to realize that both now belong to one territory. Chances are that they will become fast friends, given time to adjust and a proper introduction.

Introduce the two cats through a barrier such as a screen door or the door of a carrier. It is important that they see each other and smell each other without being able to make direct contact. A certain amount of spitting, growling, and bristling is normal, but if screams and attacking occur, allow them to smell each other but not see each other. This is best accomplished by a periodic switching of the rooms they are in. In any event, discourage any aggressive behavior by using a loud noise or squirt gun. Try not to frighten the new kitten if it is timid. When the two cats no longer react to each other, it is probably safe to let them come into direct contact (Hart, 1977).

If the two cats are different in age or size, be alert for rough play. Usually the older cat will try to establish its superiority; if so, they may have to be separated unless they are supervised.

New Abys, incidentally, should be examined by a veterinarian and quarantined before introduction into a cattery.

The above method of introduction as described also can be used to introduce your Aby to a canine member of the family. Most Abys readily adjust to a dog, assuming the dog is gentle with cats and the cats have a safe area in which to retreat.

Children should be educated in the proper care and handling of the new family addition. Demonstrate how to carry the kitten correctly (by taking hold of the kitten with one hand under its rib cage while lifting its body under its rear paws with the other hand, and holding the kitten firmly against one's hip in the crook of one's arm). Most children are just not aware that a kitten can be hurt if it is carried improperly. Abyssinians, like most cats, will avoid quick movements and loud noises, so it is wise to teach children how to handle a kitten or cat gently and calmly.

Toys

One of the most endearing qualities of Abyssinians is the way both kittens and adults totally abandon themselves during play. They leap incredibly high into the air, do back flips and somersaults, and stalk with the intensity of a lion in the jungle. (Entertaining a group of Abys with a simple button on a string has provided me with more enjoyment than almost anything else.) In addition, exercise during play is guaranteed to make your kitten healthier and happier.

Some of the best toys can be easily made at home. A wad of crumpled paper, a completely knotted pair of nylon hose, or a feather hung from a string are examples; however, always supervise your Aby when it plays with homemade toys to ensure all is well and that your kitten or cat does not hurt itself. Never offer rubber bands or string to an unsupervised cat, as it often will eat such material, and this can lead to the serious problem of intestinal blockage.

Pet shops carry numerous toys that are safe and satisfying for your cat. If you purchase toys that have springs, bells, squeakers, or any other small part that could easily detach and be swallowed, be certain to remove all dangerous parts before letting your cat play with them. Watch out for toys with paint that can flake and, thus, be consumed.

Manners

To an Abyssinian kitten, all the world is a toy; however, there are some things you may consider off limits. These could include climbing your curtains, walking on the kitchen table and counters, begging for food, or eating your favorite house plants. The kitten should have learned the basics of good behavior before you brought it home, but these basics must be reinforced and expanded to develop the kind of pet you want.

It is important to be consistent when enforcing rules for your kitten. If something is not acceptable behavior one day, then it always must be unacceptable. To punish for something one day and not punish the next will only result in confusion for the kitten, not in better manners. Do not expect overnight results.

A squirt gun filled with water is a good deterrent, as it is not easily associated with you (Hart, 1979). A stern lecture in a loud voice is also a good method.

Training

Cats can be trained, but you cannot rely on them to perform on cue. The easiest thing to teach is to "come" when called.

Most pet shops stock a variety of toys that are safe for cats. Always check to see that the toys you offer your Abyssinian have no dangling strings that could strangle the cat or any loose parts that could be swallowed by your pet.

One wonders what kind of reward or treat is in store for this group of well-behaved felines! Breeders: Bob and Patty Taylor.

Start by asking the kitten to come only a short distance when you call its name. Reward it promptly with a treat. The expectation of a reward is very important in the training process. (Note how quickly the kitten learns the sound of a can opener or the refrigerator door!) Gradually increase the distance until your kitten will come to you from any part of the house. This method also will teach a kitten its name.

Next, Abys can be trained to fetch. They will naturally follow a thrown paper ball or other toy. As soon as the cat has the toy in its mouth, call it to you and reward it with a treat. Fetching seems to be great fun, and eventually the cat will not need to be rewarded.

Walking on a leash with a cat is quite an experience and fairly easy to teach your cat to do. You will need to purchase a light-weight leash and harness. The best harness is a "figure eight" style which is made especially for cats, as a dog harness will not work. A collar is not as safe; your cat may slip out of a collar. Fit the harness snugly so that not even a frightened cat would be able to escape. Let the cat adjust to the harness by wearing it around the house. No matter how much of a fuss your cat makes at first, it will become accustomed to it. Next, attach the leash and follow the cat around the house. It is this sensation of being followed that seems to be the most disturbing to the Aby. Gradually exert your will in determining the direction of the walk.

Many other tricks and commands have been taught to Abys quite easily. These include directions to sit up and beg, jump through a hoop, speak, and so forth. Training takes time, patience, and, of course, repetition.

While cats are safer and healthier when they are kept indoors, rather than outdoors, there are several dangers inside the home against which precautions must be taken. Many houseplants, for instance, are poisonous to cats. Check with your veterinarian, with a local garden center, or with a plant identification book to find out which plants are safe, and which are not, to keep around the house.

Health and Safety

by Kenna L. Mawk, D.V.M. and Kate Faler

A healthy Abyssinian is a joy to behold. It is alert and inquisitive. Its natural intelligence is apparent to all who become acquainted with this breed. The eyes should be bright and clear, and free of film or matter. Your Aby should be active and playful. The coat should gleam and feel soft and lustrous to the touch. The body should be firm and muscular—neither obese nor thin and bony.

The purpose of this chapter is to provide both pet owner and breeder with some guidelines for maintaining a healthy, happy cat. It is not intended to be a substitute for your veterinarian. He or she is the best friend your Aby has.

The section on specific diseases is meant to give basic background knowledge and to emphasize preventive medicine. Medical knowledge and procedures change with continuing research; thus, your veterinarian always should be the final authority on your pet's health.

Cat-Proofing Your Home

Abyssinians truly are an alert and inquisitive breed. They insist on examining every part of their environment and supervising even minute changes. Before bringing your new cat home, walk through the house room by room, especially the basement and attic, looking for escape routes. Abys have been lost, and recovered after much effort, up chimneys, through furnace ducts via a loose grate, and inside acoustical ceilings. Remember, your cat will have nothing to do all day but challenge any and all small, interesting openings.

Cupboards containing cleaning solvents, paints, insecticides, and the like should be locked tightly, preferably with a hook and eye, as magnetic catches sometimes are opened by ingenious Abys. Brooms should be locked away, as they are apt to be chewed by your Aby, and deaths have been caused by a piece of straw puncturing an internal organ.

Threaded needles are a hazard, and sewing baskets should be kept closed and put away. Many a cat has swallowed the thread while playing with it. The accompanying needle follows, catching in the mouth or throat or passing into the stomach, where it may puncture or cause other severe internal problems.

Electrical cords can be treated with bitter flavors such as apple, oil of clove, or hot pepper. Place the solution on a cotton ball and run it up and down the cords. It is effective, for most Abys, up to a year.

Your fireplace should be supplied with a screen, and likewise, any exposed heating element should be protected. Cats should not be allowed on the stove at any time.

Other appliances also can be dangerous. The lid on a top-loading dishwasher, if left open, might accidentally fall closed on the cat. And many a cat has tried to slip into the refrigerator for a snack past its sleepy-eyed owner. This can be a very unpleasant experience, as the insulation acts as soundproofing and it may be a while before the mistake is discovered. Washers and dryers seem to be especially attractive as places to sleep, so it is best to make a habit of keeping them closed.

Drowning in a toilet bowl or uncovered aquarium has occurred. Normally an Aby would be able to climb out, but panic could result in a blow to the head causing unconsciousness and tragedy. Most Abys like drinking out of the toilet bowl, so if you usually leave the lid open, avoid the continual type of bowl cleaners which are dispensed with each flush, as they can be toxic.

When a kitten is young, it is best to shuffle your feet when walking, especially in the dark. Adult Abyssinians, however, learn to keep out from under foot.

These are just a few of the hazards to be aware of around the house. Careful consideration of the cat's point of view may reveal other hazards.

Many dwellings are beautifully decorated inside and out with a wide variety of plants and shrubs. Unfortunately, some of these are poisonous to cats. The following table lists some of the more common ones. If you are not sure what kind you have, ask at a greenhouse or consult a plant identification book.

Amaryllis (*Amaryllis* spp.)
Autumn crocus (*Colchicum autumnale*)
Avocado (*some varieties*) (*Persea americana*)
Bittersweet (*Celastrus* spp.)
Black-eyed Susan (*Rudbeckia* spp.)
Bleeding heart (*Dicentra spectabilis*)
Jimsonweed, Thornapple (*Datura metel*)
Larkspur, Delphinium (*Delphinium* spp.)
Laurels (*Kalmia* spp.)
Lily-of-the-valley (*Convallaria majalis*)
Lobelia, Cardinal Flower (*Lobelia* spp.)
Lupine, Bluebonnet (*Lupinus* spp.)
Box hedge (*Buxus sempervirens*)
Candelabra cactus (*Euphorbia lactea*)
Castor bean (*Ricinus communis*)
Christmas rose (*Helleborus niger*)
Crown-of-thorns (*Euphorbia millii*)

MONKSHOOD, ACONITE
(*Aconitum* spp.)

PRIVET
(*Ligustrum vulgare*)

YEW
(*Taxus* spp.)

Daffodil, Narcissus (*Narcissus* spp.)
Daphne (*Daphne* spp.)
Dumbcane (*Dieffenbachia* spp.)
Flax (*Linum usitatissimum*)
Foxglove (*Digitalis purpurea*)
Horse chestnut (*Aesculus hippocastanum*)
Hyacinth (*Hyacinthus orientalis*)
Hydrangea (*Hydrangea* spp.)
Iris (*Iris* spp.)
Ivy, English and Baltic (*Hedrea helix*)
Jerusalem cherry (*Solanum pseudocapsicum*)
Marigold, Marsh marigold (*Caltha palustris*)
Mistletoe (*Phoradendron flavescens*)
Monkshood, Aconite (*Aconitum* spp.)
Oleander (*Nerium oleander*)
Philodendron (*Philodendron* spp.)
Poinsettia (*Euphorbia pulcherrima*)
Poppy (*Papaver* spp.)
Potato, unripe tuber and sprouts from tubers
    (*Solanum tuberosum*)
Privet (*Ligustrum vulgare*)
Rhododendron (*Rhododendron* spp.)
Rhubarb (*Rheum rhaponticum*)
Snowdrop (*Galanthus nivalis*)
Snow-on-the-mountain (*Euphorbia marginata*)
Tansey (*Tanacetum vulgare*)
Tobacco, flowering (*Nicotiana tabacum*)
Virginia creeper (*Parthenocissus quinquefolia*)
Wisteria (*Wisteria* spp.)
Yew (*Taxus* spp.)

Sanitation

Proper sanitation is essential in order to maintain the health of your Aby. Litter boxes (or pans) should be scooped out daily. Frequent changes of litter, along with thorough cleaning and disinfection of the litter box, is necessary. Food and water dishes should be washed daily. Bedding should be kept clean.

Disinfectants are important in maintaining proper sanitation; however, some disinfectants have the potential to be toxic to cats. Cats are very sensitive, for example, to phenol compounds. With *any* disinfectant, take care to provide ample ventilation. Also, be sure that all cleaned surfaces are completely dry before allowing your Abyssinian to come in contact with them. Cats can ingest the disinfectant (which, when wet can stick to the cat's fur) as they lick and groom themselves. Many products, however, are effective disinfectants and have been used safely with the proper precautions.

Recent studies have shown that liquid bleach in a 1:64 dilution (one-fourth cup per gallon of water) is one of the more effective disinfectants against some of the most common viruses.

Isolation

If you have a multiple-cat household, it is very important to isolate new and/or ill cats. The isolation area should be completely separated from contact with the other cats in the household. Food bowls, water dishes, and litter pans should be disposable. Disinfect your hands after touching the cat, and wear an apron (which can be left in isolation) or avoid holding the cat against your clothes. When a cat is removed from isolation, disinfect the area completely and leave it closed off for at least four days.

Medical Records

It is important that you keep an accurate medical history of your cat. This will be of great value to both you and your veterinarian. Include dates and types of vaccinations, wormings, and laboratory test results. Write a brief paragraph whenever your cat is sick. Note your observations and the veterinarian's diagnosis and treatment. If you are breeding Abyssinians, you may wish to add dates of heat cycles, breedings, and births.

Signs of Illness

One of the best reasons to keep your cat indoors is that it can be observed often and treated for illness if need be. Sometimes it is difficult to detect when cats are sick because they show few symptoms until the condition is serious. Be alert for any of the following changes.

Appetite loss: Skipping one meal is not serious, but if your cat refuses its formerly favorite treat or consistently refuses food for longer than 24 hours, it is cause for concern.

Cloudy or mattery eyes: The eyes often reflect a cat's general state of health. Excessive tearing or discharge, redness, and swelling may be seen and could be a sign of viral or bacterial infection, allergies, or a foreign body. A scratch or ulcer on the cornea may cause the eye to become slightly opaque, although many times a special stain must be applied by your veterinarian in order to detect such an injury.

Lump: Any lump should be checked by your veterinarian, especially if it increases in size or if the cat shows other signs of illness.

Pain: To determine if your cat is in pain, look for signs of restlessness, discomfort when touched, or change in routine. For example, a cat that normally chews dry food with pleasure and now prefers canned food may have a sore mouth.

Scooting on the rear end: This is not necessarily diagnostic of worms as is commonly believed. More likely it indicates impaction of the anal glands. These are fluid-filled sacs on each side of the rectum which normally empty during defecation. Other causes might be irritation of the anus, or a foreign body.

Increase or decrease of water consumption: A decrease in liquid consumption can lead to dehydration, especially if fever, vomiting, and/or diarrhea is present. Check for dehydration by picking up a loose fold of the cat's skin (the neck is a good place) and letting it go. Normally the skin will spring back into shape. The amount of dehydration can be estimated by how quickly the skin returns to its original position. Water loss is a very dangerous problem in kittens. Excessive fluid intake, on the other hand, may indicate an infection, diabetes, or kidney or bladder infection.

Vomiting: Cats normally purge themselves of indigestible material, like hairballs, through vomiting. Gulping of food, especially dry food, occasionally seems to cause regurgitation. However, if the vomiting occurs frequently and/or the vomit contains mucus or blood, has a bad odor, or is off-color, consult your veterinarian.

Frequent urination or straining: Often this indicates the presence of a bladder infection. This is a particular problem in males as they develop a blockage due to the relatively small size of the penis and urethra. Straining, bloody urine, and frequent trips to the litter pan are serious symptoms and should be treated as an emergency.

Diarrhea: This may be due to a mild upset from dietary causes or diarrhea may be a sign of a more serious illness. Many cats as adults cannot digest milk, and this is a frequent cause of diarrhea. Other possibilities might include viral, bacterial, or parasitic infections, intestinal foreign bodies, or metabolic disturbances, to mention a few. Fresh blood in the stool is suggestive of bleeding in the large intestine or colon, while a black, tarry color is indicative of bleeding in the stomach or small intestine. The color of the stool also varies with the type of diet given.

Straining to defecate: Straining could be a sign of constipation or of a foreign body in the cat's system. Many owners mistake straining to urinate as constipation; however, the position assumed by the cat is slightly different.

Respiratory distress: Gasping, mouth breathing, rapid respiration, and difficult respiration are all signs of illness and may indicate a respiratory infection, anemia, metabolic problems, or viral infection. Any time breathing is interfered with, it is an emergency and your veterinarian should be consulted immediately.

Vaginal discharge: Any kind of vaginal discharge in your female Aby should be investigated by your veterinarian.

Dullness of the hair coat: This is a general symptom that indicates the cat is not feeling well. The skin and hair can reflect many systemic diseases; nutritional deficiencies, parasites, or low-grade infections are some causes. External parasites, allergies, or skin infections, for example, may produce such problems as flaky skin, loss of hair, or they may produce an oily texture to the hair coat.

Other Vital Signs

The normal respiration rate for cats is 26 breaths per minute. The easiest way to determine your Aby's respiration rate is to watch the rise and fall of its chest. Each inhaling plus exhaling motion is one count. Count for 15 seconds and multiply by four, or for 30 seconds and multiply by two to get the one-minute rate.

The color of the cat's gums is an excellent indication of shock, anemia, and/or level of oxygen. Become familiar with the normal pink color of your Aby's gums so that you will be able to detect a change toward blue or white, should this occur. The change in gum color is a valuable piece of information for your veterinarian, should you need to contact him or her by telephone.

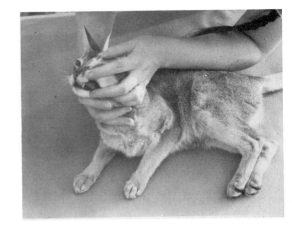

Periodically check the color of the mucus membrane, which, normally, should be pink.

Restraint

Most Abys are calm and docile and require a minimum of restraint. When restraint of your cat is necessary, to administer medicine, for example, apply as little force as possible to get the job done, as cats often meet force with force. Throughout the procedure, pet and reassure your cat, but do not let your guard down. Cats are intermittent strugglers and seem to know when you relax. Some will use angry screaming or growling as an intimidation tactic. If your restraint is effective, ignore the complaints.

Cats are among the hardest animals to restrain, especially lithe and muscular Abyssinians. You must keep track of five potential weapons—the teeth and four sets of claws. Clipping the claws before restraining your cat will minimize damage, should things get out of control.

Wrapping the cat in a large, non-bulky towel and holding the wrapped cat on your lap is effective. Wrap the towel around the cat's body in a cocoon-like fashion. The ends of the towel should be on the top of the cat. The most important area of the towel to grip firmly is the folds around the neck, as the first thing the Aby will try to do is to push its front feet out.

When carrying a cat, hold it in the crook of your arm with the front feet between the fingers of the same arm. Press the cat's hind end tightly against your side with your elbow to control the back feet. This leaves a free hand to open doors or further restrain the head by holding the cat under the chin or by the scruff of the neck. Although this carry position can be very effective, always use a carrier or harness and leash when you go outside.

Use the same position for restraint on a counter top or table, but lean your upper body across the cat. If it struggles, apply weight to pin it down. This is especially effective when taking the cat's temperature.

If you fear your Aby might bite (few do unless injured or very frightened), a muzzle can be made from a strip of cloth or gauze. The cat's front feet must be held once the muzzle is in

Two methods of how to properly carry a cat. The hind legs are restrained by "pinning" them against one's body with one's elbow. Using the other hand, one can restrain the cat's head by supporting it under the chin (above) or by grasping the loose folds of skin at the nape of the cat's neck (below).

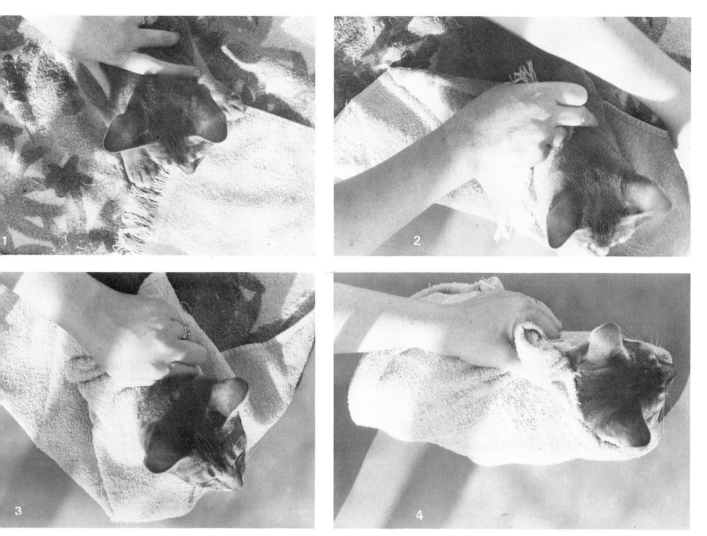

An effective way to restrain a cat (in order to administer medication, for example) is to wrap it "cocoon style" in a large, non-bulky towel. First, spread out a towel on top of a table and fold back one of the corners. Place the cat on the towel near the edge of the folded corner (1). Next, bring up the other three corners in much the same way as you would a baby's diaper, making certain the folds are securely wrapped so that the cat cannot squirm out of this enclosure (2 and 3). Now firmly grasp all of the towel ends, which should be on top of the cat (4). The wrapped cat can then be examined or given medication.

position to prevent its removal. Take a two-foot-long strip and tie a loop in the middle with a simple overhand knot. Slip this loop over the cat's nose so that the knot is under the chin. Bring the ends around behind the ears and tie with another simple overhand knot. Take one of the free ends and bring it down across the forehead and thread it through the loop around the nose. Bring this end back up between the ears to tie a bow knot with the other end for quick release.

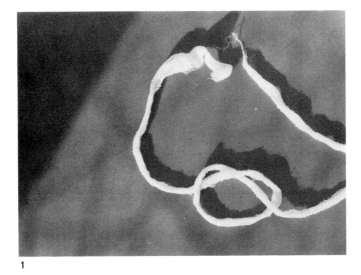

1

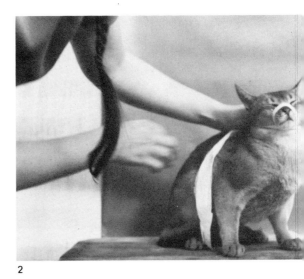

2

4

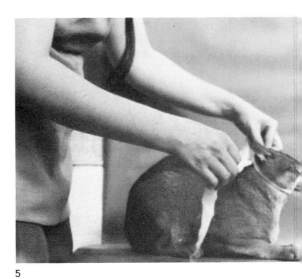

5

7

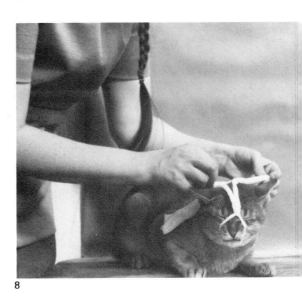

8

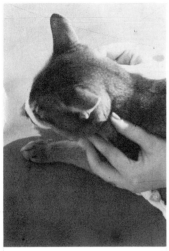

3

6

When administering first aid, it might be necessary to first tie a muzzle around your cat's jaws to prevent it from biting you. (Rarely will this happen with Abys, but it is better not to take a chance.) Using a two-foot strip of cotton fabric or cotton gauze, tie a loop in the middle with a simple overhand knot (1), then slip the loop over the cat's nose so that the knot is under the chin (2 and 3). Bring the ends around behind the cat's ears (4) and tie the ends together with another overhand knot (5). Take one of the free ends and bring it down across the cat's forehead and slip it through the loop that is around the cat's nose (6). Bring this end back up between the cat's ears (7) to tie a bow knot with the other end (8 and 9). *Note:* A bow knot is used so that the muzzle can be quickly removed.

9

Taking the Temperature

Whenever illness is suspected in your cat, the quickest means of determining the cat's condition and, perhaps, the cause, is to take its temperature with a thermometer. As a general rule, the more serious the infection, the higher the cat's temperature will be. An abnormally low temperature may indicate shock.

There are two types of mercury thermometers available: oral and rectal. Both measure temperature in exactly the same way; however, do not use the oral thermometer. Rectal thermometers are recommended. They are inexpensive and rather small (they are used for babies) and can be purchased in most drugstores.

When using a mercury thermometer, shake the column of mercury down below normal temperature by holding on to the top of the thermometer and snapping the wrist with a sharp downward motion. A subsequent colder temperature will not cause the thermometer to read below a previous higher temperature; it must be shaken down. Lubricate the tip of the thermometer with a lubricating agent such as *plain* petroleum jelly. Restrain the cat (you might need someone to help you) and insert the thermometer into the cat's anus with a gentle twisting motion. It is important that the thermometer enter the rectum about one-third the length of the thermometer in order to record an internal rather than an external body temperature. Hold the thermometer and the cat's tail together so that if one moves, so does the other. Leave it in place for one and one-half minutes, then gently withdraw it, wipe it off, and read the temperature.

Note that the mercury thermometer is triangle-shaped. One side is colored, one has numbers, and the third side has lines. In order to accurately read the thermometer, hold it so that you are looking at the edge of the triangle that is between the lined and numbered sides. Slowly rotate the thermometer between your fingers until you can see the wide silver column of mercury. Each mark on the thermometer is two-tenths of a degree (0.2°). The average normal temperature for a cat is 101.5° F., ranging from 101 to 102° F. If the cat was excited during the process, the temperature might have elevated to 102.5° F., but anything above that would be considered a fever.

Taking the Pulse

The pulse often can be an indication of internal conditions, especially in cases of injury. It is taken from the femoral artery, which runs between the two large muscle masses on the inside of each hind leg. Gently place your hand in this area and rotate it back and forth to locate the division between the muscles and then the artery. Place your index and middle fingers over the vessel. Do not press too hard; the blood supply will be cut off. Count the beats for 15 seconds and multiply by four, or for 30 seconds and multiply by two, to get the one-minute rate. The

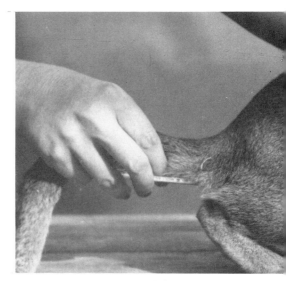

Be certain to use a rectal thermometer when taking a cat's temperature. In order to take an accurate internal temperature, the thermometer must be inserted into the anal opening and left in place for 1½ minutes.

A cat's pulse rate can easily be determined by using one's index and middle fingers and pressing them together against the femoral artery (just inside the cat's back leg).

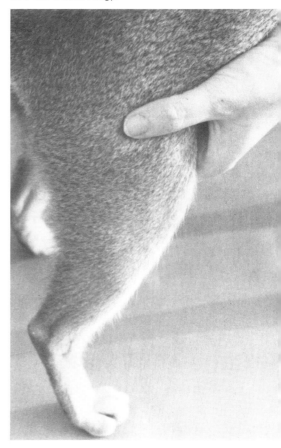

normal rate is 110-140 beats per minute (average 120). It is a good idea to practice this until you are proficient before the need arises to use the skill.

Medications

If a sick cat is to become well again, it is essential that all medications be given *exactly as prescribed* by the veterinarian. The following techniques will aid you in speeding your cat's recovery. After each treatment, pet and reassure your patient so that some reward is associated with the process.

Pills: There are some Abyssinians who can be fooled by your hiding a pill in a piece of hamburger or cheese, but for the majority, the medication must be forced down the throat. If tablets must be divided into doses, use a sharp knife to cut each tablet into pieces as equal as possible. Coating the pill with butter sometimes will make it go down more easily.

It is wise to have an assistant hold your cat's front paws while you administer the medication, but if this is not possible, restrain the cat, as described previously, by wrapping it in a large towel and holding the cat on your lap facing you. Place your palm over the cat's skull between its ears. Next, grasp its head firmly with your thumb and middle finger. Now tilt the cat's head way back so that you can look down its throat in order to position the pill correctly. Holding the pill between the thumb and index finger of your hand while pulling open the lower jaw with the middle finger of the same hand, drop the pill as far back into the cat's throat as you can and give the pill a little push with your index finger. (While doing this, of course, keep the cat's lower jaw open with your middle finger.) Once the pill is deep in the cat's throat, hold the cat's mouth closed and stroke its throat. Offer praise to your patient. When the cat licks its nose, the pill has been swallowed.

Liquid: Always shake medicine containers thoroughly and use a standardized measuring device. A syringe with the needle removed is the best tool to use, as it reduces waste; however, a small bottle, spoon, or plastic eyedropper also can be used successfully. Syringes can be obtained from your veterinarian or from a feed store.

Restrain your cat (wrapped in a large towel) and hold it on your lap facing you, unless you can get someone to help you hold the cat in place. Pull open the cat's lip just behind the canine tooth (fang) and insert the tip of the syringe, spoon, or whatever you choose to use. The cat should open its mouth when it feels the pressure. If it does not open its mouth, place the palm of your hand over the cat's ears (as in giving a pill) and gently squeeze the corners of the mouth. After dispensing the liquid, hold the cat's mouth closed and stroke its throat until the liquid has

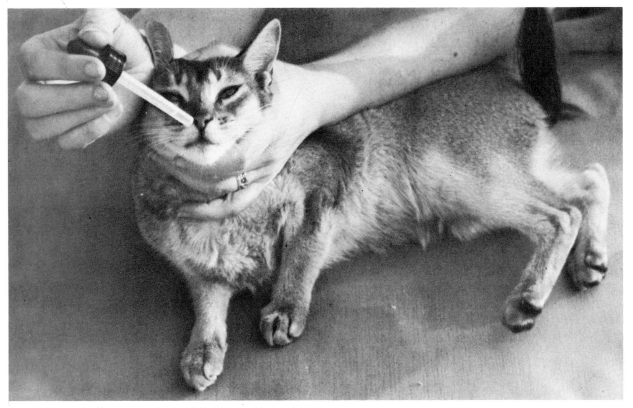

been swallowed. DO NOT TILT THE CAT'S HEAD BACK AND POUR THE LIQUID IN, AS IT CAN BE IN-HALED.

Semi-solid or gel: Squeeze the specified amount onto your finger, open the cat's mouth, and quickly spread it on the roof of the mouth.

Ear preparations: First carefully clean the outside of the cat's ear with damp cotton or a paper towel wrapped around your finger. Retain a good grip on the cat's head while squeezing the medication into the ear canal. Next, with your thumb and index finger on either side of the base of the ear, massage in a pinching motion. This is essential to spread the medication deep into the ear. The cat will flip out any excess when you let go of its head.

Eye ointment: Ointment is often used in the eye instead of drops because it lasts longer. Place your palm over the ear on the affected side and reach around with your thumb and index finger until you can stretch the skin above and below the eyelids to open them. Apply a line of ointment across the eye surface, then close the eye and massage gently.

Eye drops: Hold the cat's head and eyelids as previously described. Steady the other hand containing the dropper by resting it on the cat's head. Do not move the dropper close to the eye surface as a sudden movement by your patient could be disastrous.

Nose drops: Tilt the cat's head up and apply a drop to each nostril. Allow the liquid to flow in.

When administering nose drops, tilt the cat's head back to ensure the preparation reaches the nasal passageways.

It is important to keep a cat's head very steady while applying eye drops to an injured or infected eye.

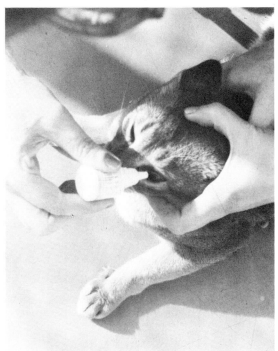

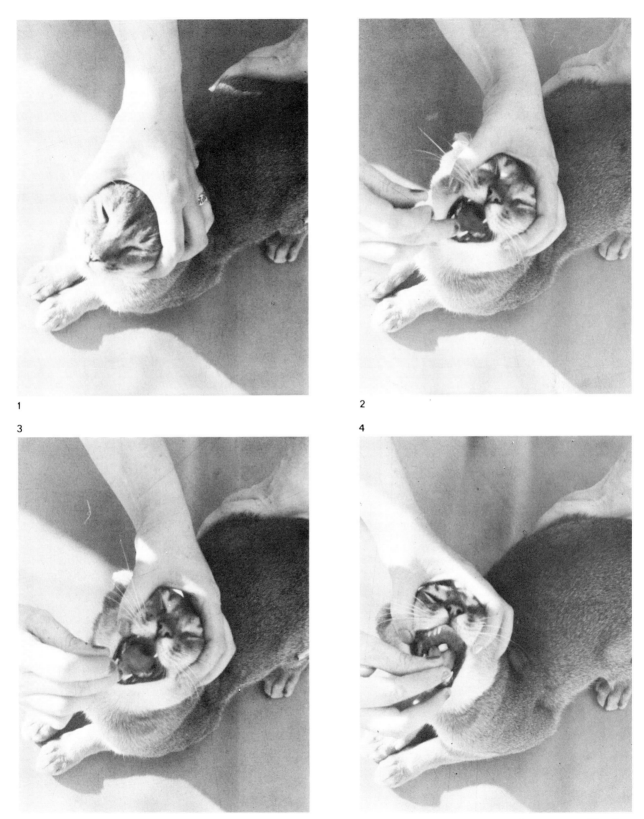

1

2

3

4

The best way to make certain a cat swallows a pill is to place the pill far back in the cat's throat yourself rather than to hide the pill in the cat's food. Grasp the cat's head with one hand so that your index finger rests on one corner of the cat's mouth and your thumb rests on the other corner (1). Tilt the cat's head back and pull the lower jaw down with the middle finger of your other hand while holding the pill (2). With the cat's mouth fully open (3), place the pill far back on the cat's tongue and give it a push with your index finger (4). Close the cat's mouth, holding it shut with your hand, and stroke the cat's throat with your other hand. Wait until you see the cat swallow to be sure the mission was successful.

First Aid

For the most part, you should leave the job of diagnosis and treatment to your veterinarian. If your Abyssinian is sick, delaying treatment by the use of home remedies may reduce its chances for recovery. However, there are times when a veterinarian cannot be reached or when a minor problem can be corrected. The purpose of this section is to provide you with some basic procedures to make your pet more comfortable and prevent further complications until medical care can be obtained.

Never use a medication that was previously prescribed for another problem without checking with your veterinarian first. In many cases more harm than good has been done by giving an inappropriate drug.

Never give aspirin to your cat unless your veterinarian instructs you to do so. Aspirin can be used safely (Aronson, 1975); however, cats are *very* sensitive to this drug, and the proper dose is essential. It is usually recommended only as a temporary measure and some veterinarians do not recommend it in any situation.

Minor abrasions and cuts: Minor abrasions and cuts should be cleaned with hydrogen peroxide or a mild soap and water. Avoid using alcohol to clean wounds. An antibiotic ointment or first aid cream, which is available at the drugstore, may be applied. Puncture wounds and deep or large cuts may be treated in this manner until your veterinarian can be consulted. A bandage may be applied to keep the wound clean. If excessive bleeding is present, apply pressure directly over the wound to stop the flow of blood.

Eye irritations: Inflamed eyes can be soothed by using a mild eyewash or plain water that has been sanitized by being boiled and then cooled. One teaspoon of table salt added to one pint of boiled water makes an excellent eyewash. Again, these are only temporary measures. Persistent or severe problems require examination by your veterinarian.

Eye injuries: Severe eye injuries from trauma, penetrating foreign bodies, or protrusion or swelling of the eyeball should be considered emergencies. In case a chemical irritant gets into your Abyssinian's eyes, first flush the eyes immediately with plenty of water and then consult your veterinarian. Speed in washing the irritant out is essential.

Diarrhea: Simple diarrhea due to a change in diet or water may be alleviated by administering a coating agent such as Kaopectate®. The dose for an adult cat is one teaspoon three to four times daily. It is also helpful to provide a bland diet for a few days. Such a diet consists of boiled rice mixed with boiled hamburger or chicken. Be sure to remove the fat. Strained baby food such as chicken, beef,

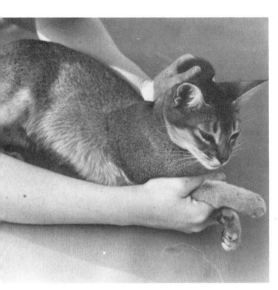

Two methods of restraining a cat for treatment and/or medical examination. Grasp the front paws with one hand, while holding the loose folds of skin at the nape of the neck with the other hand (above) or by holding the cat's head underneath the chin with the other hand (below). The hind feet can be further controlled by leaning one's upper body against the cat in order to "pin" it to the table.

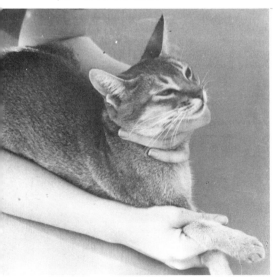

lamb, or veal is easy to digest, and most cats consider it a special treat. Persistent or severe diarrhea should be investigated by your veterinarian.

Constipation: Hard fecal material may be softened by placing one-half teaspoon of mineral oil in the cat's food. Do not give mineral oil directly, as it may be inhaled into the lungs and this may result in pneumonia.

Vomiting: If your Abyssinian is vomiting and does not seem to be able to keep anything in its stomach, the best thing to do is to remove all food and water. In most cases, attempting to "put something in the stomach" only makes the situation worse. Your veterinarian should be consulted as soon as possible.

Minor burns: For minor burns, a first aid cream or antibiotic ointment may be applied. Cold water or ice compresses may be applied to more severe burns. Veterinary aid should be obtained as quickly as possible. Shock, infection and fluid loss are life-threatening complications in the case of severe burns.

Cold temperatures: Exposure to freezing temperatures may result in frostbite to the ears, tail, and legs of your Aby. Warm the affected areas with moist heat packs; do not rub, apply pressure, or put ointments on those areas. Take your cat to the veterinarian for further care. In cases of prolonged exposure to cold, a subnormal body temperature (hypothermia) can develop. Apply a heating pad set on a *low* temperature to the affected areas, or give your Aby a warm bath. In cases of hypothermia, medical aid should be obtained immediately, as shock and kidney failure are complicating factors.

Heat stroke: Never leave your Abyssinian in a locked parked car during the summer months. The temperature inside the car can rise to as high as 120°F. in just a few minutes. Your cat can sustain a body temperature of 107 to 109°F. for only a short time before permanent brain and circulatory damage occurs. In the event of heat stroke, give your cat cold baths, either in a tub or with a spray. Massage and flex the cat's legs. Get medical aid immediately.

Foreign bodies: Foreign bodies or obstructions within the respiratory tract that interfere with breathing are emergencies. Keep calm and keep the cat as calm and quiet as possible, as excitement will only aggravate the respiratory distress. Seek veterinary aid as quickly as possible.

Poison: If your pet has swallowed a poison, vomiting may be induced by giving one teaspoon of hydrogen peroxide or one teaspoon of salt on the back of the tongue. **Do not** induce vomiting if an unknown or corrosive material such as an acid, an alkali, or kerosene has been ingested or if the cat is unconscious or in a convulsion. In the case of external contact with a poison or corrosive material, wash the area with profuse amounts of water. Get your Abyssinian to a veterinarian as soon as possible.

Convulsions: Poisoning, encephalitis, head injuries, and epilepsy are some causes of convulsions. The cat should be confined in a blanket to prevent it from hurting itself or others. Do not attempt to give any medication or place any object in the cat's mouth. Consult your veterinarian.

In the event your Abyssinian is seriously injured, speed in obtaining medical aid is essential. You should have the phone number of your veterinarian listed with other emergency numbers by your telephone. Also list the number of the local veterinary emergency clinic and/or poison control center if your town has one.

Keep your pet warm and as quiet as possible. Cats are very susceptible to shock, which can be more of a threat to life than the actual injury.

No matter how docile and affectionate your Abyssinian may normally be, when hurt and frightened, it may bite and scratch. Take precautions to protect yourself. A heavy towel or blanket may be used to restrain the cat (see "Restraint" section). It is best to place an injured animal with possible internal injuries or fractures in a small box or carrier so that it can be transported without inflicting further pain and injury.

Geriatrics

The average lifespan of a cat is 15 years. Individual factors, of course, play a role; while one cat may be "old" at ten or 12 years, another may still be going strong at 18.

There are some special problems associated with aging cats, and the purpose of this section is to alert cat owners to signs of common geriatric problems and to help them make their Abyssinians' later years more comfortable.

Senility is manifested in many ways. Often a decrease in agility is noticeable. Aging cats may have difficulty controlling urination and defecation; therefore, several easily accessible litter boxes should be provided throughout the house. Another obvious sign is that aging cats may neglect grooming themselves, so their owners must take over by combing, brushing, and bathing them. The cat's claws may become long due to less exercise and degeneration of the elastic ligament which normally keeps the claws pulled back into their sheaths. Regular clipping of the claws is necessary. Older cats tend to become thin and frail for no apparent reason, and, thus, require extra warmth. Food that is offered should be easy to digest and highly nutritious. Vitamin supplements often are recommended for aging cats.

Accumulation of dental plaque and tartar is a common problem. Infections of the teeth and gums follow, causing loss of teeth and providing a source of infection for other parts of the body. Regular cleaning of the teeth and extraction of infected teeth are essential.

Kidney failure is a frequent cause of death in an old cat. Signs of kidney disease include excessive thirst coupled with production of large amounts of urine, loss of appetite, and—as the disease progresses—vomiting and diarrhea. Diagnosis is by means of testing blood chemistries and urinalysis. Damage to the kidneys cannot be reversed; however, changes in diet, vitamins, and antibiotics may be used to limit further damage and it is hoped, lengthen your Aby's life.

Diabetes mellitus is seen most frequently in cats over eight to ten years of age. Signs are excessive thirst and urination and loss of weight. Blood tests are required for diagnosis. If a cat is in good health otherwise, it is possible to treat diabetes with insulin injections and dietary management. Most owners are capable of learning to give the necessary daily injections.

Heart and liver problems are manifested by weight loss, loss of appetite, nausea, and depression. Cats are particularly prone to cerebral-vascular accidents similar to a stroke in humans. Loss of coordination, circling, and convulsions may be seen.

The aging cat is more likely to develop cancerous growths. Unspayed older female cats have a tendency to develop mammary tumors and uterine infections. Females that are not to be used for breeding should be spayed, preferably before old age and disease problems develop.

As your Abyssinian ages, it will become more susceptible to infection and certain diseases. It is important that the older pet have regular check-ups. Signs of disease should be reported to your veterinarian without delay.

Euthanasia

Euthanasia may be recommended for your cat when the prognosis is hopeless or when severe pain and suffering are involved. This is a difficult decision for an owner to make about a beloved pet; however, there are times when euthanasia is the most loving and responsible decision. Your veterinarian can help you weigh the pros and cons of prolonging the life of your Aby in the face of terminal disease. Usually an intravenous injection is used which is painless and takes effect immediately.

Proper attention to health and safety will ensure that your Abyssinian will be around to provide you with many years of pleasure and companionship. The domesticated cat is a devoted creature and is dependent upon its owner for proper care. It is your responsibility to see that your Aby's needs are met and that medical care is provided as needed.

Young kittens, such as this three-week-old ruddy male, are particularly susceptible to disease, and this is why it is important to have them immunized against the major cat diseases about the time they stop nursing. Kittens receive only *temporary* immunity from their mother's milk.

Some Major Cat Diseases

by Kenna L. Mawk, D.V.M. and Kate Faler

INFECTIOUS DISEASES

Panleukopenia

This disease is also referred to as feline distemper or feline infectious enteritis (FIE). It is caused by a virus which is highly contagious and frequently fatal, especially among young kittens. The onset of the disease is rapid and may cause death before any signs of illness are noticed. The virus is shed in all body secretions and can live at room temperature for up to a year. It is usually transmitted by direct contact, but dishes, cages, bedding, and the hands and clothes of the cat's handlers are also sources of infection. Recovered cats may shed the virus for long periods and thus act as carriers of the disease.

Symptoms vary in severity and include fever, vomiting, and diarrhea, all of which may lead to dehydration. During the course of the disease, the white blood cell count drops abnormally low and the patient is very susceptible to secondary infection from bacteria or other viruses. Death is usually due to severe dehydration and/or secondary infection.

Treatment includes fluids to correct dehydration, antibiotics for bacterial infection, intestinal coating agents, and drugs to control vomiting. Usually injectable fluids are given, as oral fluids tend to be vomited up.

Good nursing care is an important aid to recovery. Medication must be given as directed by your veterinarian, hand-feeding may be necessary, and warm draft-free quarters should be provided. Strict sanitation and isolation are important.

The major form of control is vaccination. Even with intensive care, the prognosis for a cat infected with distemper is guarded. Available vaccines are highly effective and relatively inexpensive, especially when compared to the cost of treating panleukopenia.

Upper Respiratory Disease Complex

This is a generalized name used to describe upper respiratory infections in the cat. These diseases are characterized by sneezing, discharge from the eyes and nose, inflammation of the eyes, and ulcers in the mouth. Any of these symptoms may be seen alone or in any combination and may range from mild to severe. Occasionally, the lower respiratory tract will be involved and pneumonia will be present. Mouth breathing can occur if the nasal passages are blocked.

These symptoms may be caused by several different agents; rhinotracheitis (commonly referred to as herpes virus) and calici virus (which has several strains) are the most common. Together these viruses are responsible for about 80% to 90% of the cases seen. The remainder of cases involving upper respiratory disease usually are caused by an organism known as chlamydia (often referred to as pneumonitis), which, in turn, often causes conjunctivitis (an inflammation of the lining of the eye). Other viruses and bacteria are responsible only occasionally.

All of these agents are highly contagious, but they usually do not cause death, except to young kittens. Transmission occurs when an affected cat sneezes, thus spraying virus-laden droplets into the air. Respiratory infections also may be spread by the contaminated hands and clothing of anyone who handles the infected cat.

Treatment is symptomatic and supportive; that is, the symptoms are alleviated and the cat is supported until its body can recover by itself. Antibiotics are administered for secondary bacterial infections, and intravenous or subcutaneous fluids are given to correct any dehydration that may be present. It is important to keep the cat's eyes and nose clear, as loss of smell can lead to difficulty in finding food. Something with a strong odor, such as fish-flavored cat food, sardines, or cheese, may help. When ulcers are present in the mouth, a soft or liquid diet may be necessary.

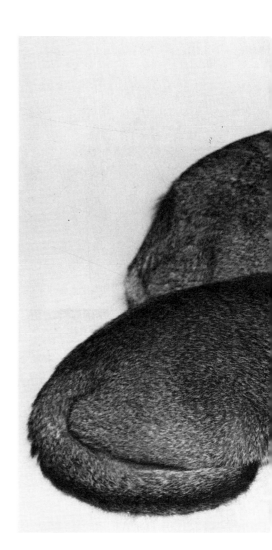

Upper respiratory diseases have become a major problem in catteries. Recently, several vaccines have been developed which protect cats against herpes virus, calici virus, and sometimes chlamydia. These are only partially effective; thus, a vaccinated cat still may exhibit signs of upper respiratory disease. These vaccines do, however, frequently prevent severe diseases from developing.

Should your Abyssinian become exposed to any of these viruses, it may become a carrier and harbor the virus in its upper respiratory passages. Stress caused by another illness, travel, giving birth, etc., often will cause the cat to "break" for a few days with signs of upper respiratory disease. Usually these signs are mild. Unfortunately, an apparently healthy cat may serve as a source of infection (a carrier) for susceptible cats or kittens. It has been estimated that the majority of cats, including those that have been vaccinated, are carriers.

Control of these diseases includes a good vaccination program. Booster shots should be given regularly to all cats. Proper sanitation and adequate ventilation in the home and/or cattery are essential, as well.

Feline Leukemia Virus (FeLV)

The feline leukemia virus was discovered in 1964. This is one of the most important disease-producing agents in felines.

A cat harboring this virus may show a variety of signs depending on the body system involved. A tumor called lymphosarcoma may develop. The most common sites are the chest cavity, kidneys, nervous system, and digestive tract. The virus may cause a true leukemia with an abnormally high number of circulating white blood cells. Quite commonly, it causes a degeneration of the blood-forming organs, resulting in anemia and/or a low white blood cell count. Reproductive problems may be seen. A cat also may carry the virus without showing any symptoms.

The leukemia virus has been shown to depress the immune system of the cat; thus, concurrent infections with other viruses or bacteria are not uncommon. A cat that shows chronic low resistance to infection should be suspected of having FeLV.

Treatment of disease caused by the leukemia virus is difficult and for the most part supports the patient while its body fights the virus itself. Blood transfusions for anemia, chemotherapy for tumors, vitamins, fluids, etc., are given. Many cats showing clinical signs of the disease die in spite of treatment, usually due to severe depression of the blood-forming organs or to secondary infection.

Studies on the occurrence of the virus have shown that most cats are exposed to the virus, have varying signs of illness, then recover and are immune; however, some cats become carriers and may show no symptoms for weeks, months, or years. Many carriers eventually develop a FeLV-related disease and progress to terminal illness (Pederson, 1979).

The virus is shed in the urine, feces, saliva, and milk of infected cats. Infection is spread by contact between infected cats and susceptible ones and may result from cats grooming each other, sharing food and litter boxes, or as a result of bites and scratches. Infection also may be spread by blood-sucking insects such as fleas, or it may pass from a mother cat to nursing offspring.

The virus is very unstable and seldom survives outside the cat for more than a few hours at room temperature. It is deactivated by most disinfectants.

There is a test available to detect the presence of the virus in the cat's bloodstream. This test involves sending a small amount of cat blood on a slide to the laboratory. A positive result indicates only the presence of the virus; it does not indicate whether a cat has a leukemia virus-associated disease or will develop a disease in the future. At times, the amount of virus present in the bloodstream can drop very low and be undetectable, thus resulting in a negative test even though the cat may be showing clinical signs of infection. Therefore, this test is only a diagnostic aid to your veterinarian, and other tests may be necessary for accurate diagnosis.

Gr. Ch. Cafra Honeysuckle and Gr. Ch. Cafra Aurora, two fine healthy specimens. Even healthy cats that have been exposed to certain viral diseases may become carriers and thus infect other feline members of the household. Check with your veterinarian about a vaccination program for your cat/cats; in most instances, vaccinations are the best form of disease prevention. Breeders: Mr. and Mrs. Lewis Fineman.

Since the level of virus in the blood may vary, a single negative test in a cat that has been previously positive does not mean that the cat has eliminated the virus. The test should be repeated several times over a four- to eight-month period to determine if true recovery has occurred (Pederson, 1979). Recently, a second test has been developed that detects the presence of FeLV antibodies in the cat's blood. This test can be performed by your veterinarian, and it is very sensitive; however, a positive result should be confirmed by the method described above.

Many breeders routinely test cats within their catteries. In order for a cattery to be considered feline leukemia virus-negative, testing must be done on all cats at periodic intervals, preferably every six months. Also, all cats that enter and leave the premises from other leukemia-free catteries should have recent negative tests as well. Cats that enter the cattery from a cattery that is *not* FeLV-negative should be tested and isolated for three months. At the end of the three month period, the test should be repeated and confirmed to be negative before introducing those cats into the cattery. In a cattery where cats test positive, the animals must be removed immediately. In order to be considered leukemia-free, it is necessary to show two completely negative tests, taken three months apart, on the remaining cats.

There has been a great deal of research done to determine if the feline leukemia virus is a potential health hazard to humans. At this time, there is no known relationship between FeLV and human cancer. Currently there is no FeLV vaccine for cats available; however, it is hoped that one may be developed in the very near future.

Feline Infectious Peritonitis

Feline infectious peritonitis is a relatively new viral disease which has been increasing in incidence since the mid-1960s. The term "peritonitis" is a misnomer, as it is really an inflammation of the tissues surrounding the blood vessels, not a true peritonitis which is an inflammation of the lining of the abdominal cavity.

Until recently, this disease was thought to be rare and invariably fatal. Current studies have shown that it is very common and that the majority of cats have been infected with the virus at some time during their lives; very few of these cats, however, develop the fatal form of the disease. The natural route of exposure and infection is still unknown.

The initial infection is mild and may produce little or no signs of disease. Many cats eliminate the virus after infection and become immune. However, some cats become carriers and are the main source of infection in nature.

A small percentage of infected cats progress to terminal illness. There are two different forms of feline infectious peritonitis. The "wet" form is characterized by fluid build-up in the abdomen or chest cavity. In these cases, diagnosis involves removing some of the fluid and analyzing its characteristics. The "dry" form of FIP is more difficult to diagnose. Areas of inflammation called granulomas form and may involve a variety of tissues, most commonly those of the liver, the kidneys, the lymph nodes, the nervous system, and the eyes. Signs of the illness may be vague, and laboratory data often are only suggestive of the disease. Only rarely has treatment of the fatal forms of FIP been successful.

Recent work by researchers has implicated that feline infectious peritonitis may possibly contribute to reproductive failures and kitten deaths within catteries (Scott, et al., 1979).

Currently, there is an FIP test available which measures antibodies in the blood. The presence of these antibodies indicates only that the cat has been exposed to the virus at some time during its life and does not tell the veterinarian if there is disease present. A high percentage of normal cats will test positive. The level of the antibodies *may* give some indication as to whether active disease is present; however, these levels are influenced by many factors. Thus, the test is subject to interpretation and must be used in conjunction with other laboratory findings and clinical signs in order to make an accurate diagnosis. Sometimes two consecutive tests are taken over a period of time to detect changes in blood levels.

There have been some efforts by a few cat breeders to establish FIP-negative catteries. At the present time, this is considered to be a futile effort, as the virus is widespread in nature (Scott, et al., 1979; Pederson, 1979). The FIP test does not differentiate between immune cats and carriers. A cattery that is having excessive deaths from FIP should look for management problems such as overcrowding, poor nutrition, inbreeding, etc. Breeding records should be studied, and breeding cats that repeatedly produce kittens who become ill with FIP should be eliminated.

At this time, there is no vaccine available. Control is aimed at sanitation and management. The virus is unstable in the environment and is sensitive to most disinfectants.

Feline Infectious Anemia

Feline infectious anemia is caused by a microorganism called *Hemobartonella felis*. This is a blood parasite and was once thought to be the most common cause of anemia in cats. However, it is now known that it represents less than 10% of the mechanisms responsible for anemia in cats. It is often seen concurrently with other infections or following stress.

The disease is transmitted by blood-sucking insects such as the flea. It is usually seen in young cats and appears to be more frequent in males. Diagnosis is made by examining a specially stained blood smear under the microscope for the presence of the organism.

Treatment involves the use of certain antibiotics to which *Hemobartonella* is sensitive, and it may include blood transfusions if the anemia is severe.

Rabies

This is a contagious viral disease that affects all warm-blooded animals, and it is almost always fatal. Cats seem to be more resistant to infection than dogs or wild animals.

The virus attacks the nervous system; therefore, the signs are those of encephalitis. Individual animals react differently but, in general, excitability and irritability followed by paralysis are seen.

The disease is usually transmitted by the bite of an infected animal; however, the chances for exposure are small if your Abyssinian is kept indoors as it should be. An effective vaccine is available and it may be required if the cat is shipped from one state to another.

Vaccines

When an animal comes into contact with a disease-causing organism such as a virus, its body recognizes this organism as foreign. Substances called antibodies are produced which neutralize or destroy the virus or bacteria. With most diseases, a type of memory system persists; should the cat be invaded by that type of organism again, within a certain period of time, the body has prepared itself to fight.

Vaccines are used to stimulate the body to build antibodies against specific diseases. Thus, these antibodies are already present should a cat subsequently be exposed to the disease against which it was vaccinated.

There are two types of vaccines available. With a killed vaccine, a dead virus is injected. Modified-live, or attenuated vaccines are prepared using a virus which has been changed so it will not cause disease; however, the virus is capable of multiplying within the body, and generally, this results in better protection for a cat than with the killed type.

Boosters are recommended for all vaccines to refresh the body's memory and keep the antibodies at a protective level. The frequency of the boosters varies with the type of vaccine.

Your veterinarian has several types of vaccines available to protect your cat against some of the major cat diseases. The vaccines are for your Abyssinian's good health. They are much less expensive than treating the diseases themselves, so it is wise to use them. The chart below can serve as a guide to vaccination programs. The actual dates vary somewhat from product to product and for individual needs.

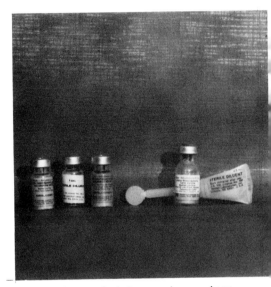

Injectable and intranasal vaccines such as these are what help cats and kittens build immunity to diseases. When a vaccine is first introduced into the cat's body, antibodies build up to fight off infection.

DISEASE	FIRST DOSE	SECOND DOSE	SUBSEQUENT BOOSTER
Feline Panleukopenia	at weaning, 8-10 weeks	3-4 weeks after first dose	1 year later/ repeated annually
Upper Respiratory	at weaning, 8-10 weeks	3-4 weeks after first dose	6 months to 1 year later/ repeat annually
Rabies	6 months	—	1-2 years later

There are several types of upper respiratory complex vaccines available. They are designed to protect against the most common and serious viruses but not against all of the ones involved. The situation is similar to the common cold in humans; because there are so many causative viruses, it is impossible to are local; thus, the virus attacks the cells lining the respiratory tract. During infection, local immune mechanisms are stimulated; however, when the vaccine virus is injected, blood antibodies are produced so they play only a partial role in local protection. Thus, when a vaccinated cat is exposed to one of the upper respiratory diseases, some signs of disease may develop. Usually, however, these signs are milder and of shorter duration than would be expected in a non-vaccinated cat.

There are some intranasal (in the nose) upper respiratory vaccines available which are given as nose and eye drops. Theoretically, this method of administration has the advantage of producing immunity at the site of virus attack and, therefore, provides more complete protection. Also, the vaccine may be given at an earlier age. With some brands, sneezing may be seen four to five days after vaccination, but this is only temporary. The intranasal vaccines have not been as widely used as the injectable types.

Although the upper respiratory vaccines are not completely protective, their use is still advocated, as they do reduce the severity of diseases seen. Abyssinians with a high risk for exposure, such as show and breeding cats, should receive boosters every six months.

OTHER DISEASES

Feline Urologic Syndrome

Although much research has been done, the exact cause of this problem remains unclear at this time and appears to be dependent upon the interaction of several factors. Several viruses have been incriminated but appear to produce disease only in conjunction with each other and/or when predisposing factors are present. Some suspected predisposing agents that have been investigated include the ash content in the cat's diet, the magnesium and phosphorus content in the diet, the type of diet, and the relationship of the diet to water balance, fluid intake, and alkaline urine. Studies have shown that early castration in males is not a factor.

In general, the disease is an inflammation of the bladder and urethra, and the usual signs are painful urination with bloody urine. The small size of the penis and urethra in male cats makes them particularly prone to this disorder. Obstruction does occur but is rare in female cats due to the relatively larger size of the female urethral opening. The inflammation results in a plug consisting of mineral crystals and/or protein material in the urethra which prevents the urine from being voided. This results in uremia, a build-up of toxic waste products in the blood, WHICH MAY LEAD TO DEATH WITHIN AS LITTLE AS 24 HOURS.

Signs of illness include frequent trips to the litter box, straining to urinate, slow urination or elimination of only small amounts of urine, and blood in the urine. If you suspect your Abyssinian has an obstruction, place your fingers on either side of its abdomen and roll the contents in your hand. In most cases, the enlarged bladder will feel like a hard lump.

Cats that exhibit signs of obstruction should be taken to the veterinarian IMMEDIATELY. Treatment usually begins with catheterization and flushing the plug out. Many veterinarians leave a catheter in place for a few days to allow some of the inflammation in the bladder and urethra to subside. If the patient is toxic and dehydrated, fluid therapy is given. Antibiotics and urinary acidifiers also are used. Most cats remain on a urinary acidifier permanently after a bout with this disease. Many veterinarians feel that dry food aggravates this condition, and they may recommend eliminating dry food from the cat's diet. Frequently, salting the cat's food is suggested to increase the cat's water consumption; this helps to dilute the urine.

Quite often affected male cats will have repeated episodes of urethral blockage. In chronic cases, a surgical procedure called a urethrostomy is recommended. This involves creating a new opening higher up where the urethra is wider; thus, the chances of obstruction are reduced. This procedure is only a means to allow cats to live with the problem; it does not cure the underlying cause.

Gingivitis

As a breed, Abyssinians seem to be prone to inflammation of the gums (gingivitis), which can lead to loss of teeth. The initiating cause is a build-up of tartar or calculus on the teeth. This, in turn, leads to inflammation complicated by bacterial infection.

Symptoms include tenderness of the gums when eating, red puffy gums which bleed when pressed, bad breath, and excessive salivation.

A complete scaling of the teeth to remove the tartar is the first step in treatment. Antibiotics (and possibly vitamins) may be prescribed. Prevention includes providing dry crunchy food or large uncooked beef bones to exercise gums and to clean the teeth, administering mouthwashes, and brushing the teeth. Periodic inspection of the Aby's teeth and gums is recommended.

Feline Acne

This is a common problem in cats and is found on the cat's chin and lips. Just as the name implies, blackheads and pustules are seen. Suggested causes are poor cleaning of the area by the cat, feeding dishes with high sides, and poorly cleaned dishes. The problem may be mild, or open sores and loss of hair may be seen.

Treatment involves cleaning the area with an antibacterial soap or alcohol and applying an antibiotic cream. In severe cases, antibiotics that treat the cat's entire system may be needed.

Hairballs

The papillae or rasps on a cat's tongue are pointed slightly backward, which necessitates the swallowing of hair during the grooming process. This hair can build up in the stomach, resulting in chronic indigestion, attempted vomiting, and even blockage requiring surgery. When a cat is troubled with hairballs, it will assume a characteristic posture. While crouching, the neck will be extended, the head will bob, and a noise sounding like a cross between a cough and a choke will be made. Treatment begins with the use of a flavored gel laxative that most Abys consider a treat. This preparation should be used routinely as a preventive measure. These hairball remedies are available in most pet shops.

Abscesses

Cats seem to be particularly prone to bacterial infection following relatively small puncture wounds. An abscess is a pocket of pus formed as a result of the infection. Cellulitis is a term used to refer to a more generalized infection which spreads through the tissues. The most common cause of abscess is a bite or a scratch from another cat.

Signs include swelling around the wound and fever, which results in listlessness and loss of appetite. After a period of time, the abscess breaks open and drains.

Treatment includes lancing, draining, and cleaning of the infected area plus the administration of antibiotics. This is an uncommon problem in cats that are kept indoors and not allowed to roam and fight outside.

Generalized Diseases Affecting the Skin

The skin reflects the general body condition and often can be affected by generalized disease. Endocrine diseases in particular, such as hypothyroidism, imbalances of sex hormones,

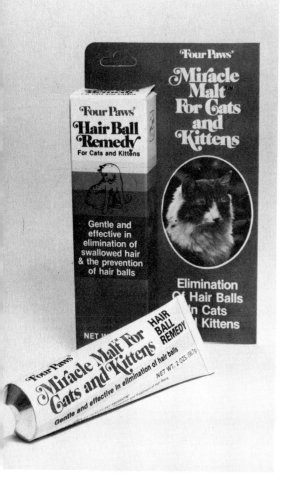

Each time your Abyssinian grooms itself by licking its fur, hair is ingested. When enough hair has been swallowed, hairballs can form in the cat's stomach and intestines where they cause great discomfort. Offer a small amount of hairball remedy regularly to your Aby to keep these wads of hair from accumulating.

and Cushing's syndrome, are responsible for hair loss and changes in the skin. Such diseases require prompt attention by your veterinarian.

Reproductive Problems

The failure of a queen to conceive, abortions, and stillbirths are reproductive problems which can be caused by a variety of factors. Occasional abortions or stillbirths from otherwise normal, healthy queens can occur and should not cause much concern; however, repeated reproductive failures from a single cat or within a cattery should be investigated by your veterinarian.

Noninfectious causes include trauma, nutritional imbalances, illness not related to pregnancy, abnormalities of the reproductive tract, psychological disturbances, exposure to toxins, abnormalities in the fetuses, and hormonal imbalance.

Viral and bacterial infections can cause abortion and stillbirth. Feline infectious peritonitis and the feline leukemia virus are commonly incriminated in reproductive failures.

Pinpointing the causes involves working closely with your veterinarian. A complete and thorough history of your queen, including management procedures, previous health problems, diet, and breeding records, should be supplied. The stage of pregnancy when abortions occur is significant.

Cultures of the queen's cervix may be taken, and blood tests to rule out FeLV and FIP will be necessary. Exploratory surgery may be an aid to diagnosis.

INTERNAL PARASITES

Internal parasites include worms and protozoans (one-celled microorganisms) which live and reproduce within a cat's body. Do not assume because worms are not visible in the stool that your cat does not have them. A microscopic examination of the cat's feces is usually necessary to diagnose most internal parasites. Diagnosis is made by identifying the parasite eggs which are passed through an infected cat's stool. A fecal exam is recommended for all kittens and it should be repeated yearly, along with a physical exam and vaccine boosters.

The practice of routine periodic worming should be performed *only* by your veterinarian, since different types of worms require different types of medication that only your veterinarian can prescribe. A fecal exam should be performed to determine if parasitic infection exists. If it does, then it is important to use the proper medication and the correct dosage, as recommended by your veterinarian, in order to eradicate the problem.

Roundworms

Occasionally roundworms may be vomited up or passed in the cat's stool. These parasites are similar in appearance to spaghetti, and they live within the cat's small intestines. One type of roundworm larva migrates through the cat's body as part of its development; in some cases, the larvae travel to the tissues in the mammary glands and, thus, may be transmitted to nursing kittens.

Transmission also occurs when a cat ingests roundworm eggs which have passed in the stool of an infected cat; therefore, sanitation is an important factor in control of the disease. Additionally, when roundworm eggs are ingested by rodents, birds, and small mammals, the larvae migrate to the body tissues where they form cysts; thus, these animals become carriers of the parasitic disease. Cats that are allowed to roam and hunt outdoors have a greater chance of becoming infected than cats that are kept indoors.

Tapeworms

Tapeworms are segmented parasites composed of a head followed by many identical segments, each of which contains sets of male and female reproductive organs. These segments become little packets of eggs and when mature are passed in the cat's stool. These worms may be seen in the feces or clinging to the hair around the cat's anus. When tapeworms are first passed, they appear as white grub-like structures which elongate and shorten as the eggs within them are emptied. Dried segments are similar in appearance to grains of uncooked rice.

Tapeworms cannot be transmitted directly from one cat to another. The eggs first must be ingested by a flea or rodent (depending on the species of tapeworm) where the larvae undergo some development. Transmission occurs when the cat eats an infected rodent or flea. Control is obtained by preventing flea infestation and by keeping your Aby indoors so it cannot hunt rodents which may carry the parasite.

Hookworms

Hookworms are very small thread-like worms which burrow into the walls of the cat's small intestine where they ingest blood. Hookworm infections are most common in areas with warm, temperate climates, as the eggs and larvae are most likely destroyed by freezing temperatures during winter months.

Hookworms are transmitted when a cat ingests the larvae; the larvae also are capable of penetrating the cat's skin. During their development, these larvae migrate through the cat's body and end up in the small intestines. Hookworms cause their damage by ingesting the cat's blood, which results in anemia. Infected cats are thin and have a rough hair coat; their stool is often black and tarry.

Eggs are passed in the cat's stool and take 58 to 66 hours of development before they are capable of infecting other cats. Since the larvae of hookworms are resistant to sunlight and drying, control is aimed at frequent removal of the cat's feces and cleaning the cat's litter box daily. Studies have shown that it is likely hookworms may be passed to nursing kittens from the milk of infected queens.

Lungworms

These worms live in the air passages and lung tissue and are not nearly as common as roundworms and tapeworms. Symptoms are coughing, poor condition, lethargy, and poor appetite. It is common for a cat to show no symptoms at all in mild infections. The eggs are coughed up and swallowed back into the gastrointestinal tract. A diagnosis may be made by examination of a stool sample.

Heartworms

There has been a lot of attention drawn to heartworms in dogs recently. Heartworm infection does occur in cats, but it is very rare.

Coccidia

Coccidia are microscopic one-celled organisms which multiply within the cells lining the intestine. As the coccidia repeatedly divide, the cells become engorged and rupture, producing inflammation and diarrhea which is often bloody. Secondary bacterial infection may complicate matters. Anemia may develop due to blood loss. Coccidia spores are passed in the cat's feces; however, they must undergo development for about 48 hours before they become infective.

Cats may be carriers without showing clinical signs and may serve as a source of infection to susceptible cats. Control is aimed at sanitation.

Toxoplasmosis

There has been a great deal of publicity concerning toxoplasmosis in cats due to its public health significance. A wide range of mammals—including humans—and birds are capable of becoming infected with this disease. Toxoplasmosis is particularly hazardous to pregnant women, as the organism can infect unborn children and cause serious disease.

Toxoplasma gondii is a small coccidia-type organism, and in the cat family it reproduces within the intestinal tract. This reproduction and subsequent shedding of the organism in the feces lasts for only seven to 14 days. In cats, as well as in other animals, a generalized infection occurs which affects various body tissues such as the liver, the lungs, the lymph nodes, the heart muscle, the skeletal muscle, the brain, and the eyes. Signs of the disease are related to the organ systems involved; however, most infections are mild without producing any signs.

Cats contract the infection by eating infected rodents, birds, or raw meat, or through contact with infected cats that are shedding the organism in their feces. Control is aimed at preventing or minimizing exposure. Your Abyssinian should be fed with meat that has been *thoroughly* heated or with dried or canned food. Litter boxes should be cleaned daily, as it takes one to five days for the organism to develop to an infective stage. (Susceptible pregnant women should wear plastic gloves while cleaning litter boxes.) Additionally, children's sandboxes should be covered (when not in use) to prevent stray cats, which might carry the disease, from eliminating in them. *Toxoplasma* can survive in soil for many months, so it is wise to wash the hands each and every time after handling the soil.

By controlling your cat's food and minimizing the chances for exposure to toxoplasmosis, your Abyssinian can be a relatively safe pet. The spread of this disease is another of the many reasons to keep your cat confined indoors. If you wish, your veterinarian can test your Abyssinian for the presence of this parasite.

EXTERNAL PARASITES

Fleas

If you live in an area where the humidity is high and winters are mild, fleas can be a major problem for you and your Abyssinian. To determine if your cat has fleas, examine the hair on the cat's neck, abdomen, and at the base of the tail. Look for black specks which are a combination of dried blood and flea feces. Small, oval, white eggs may also be seen, and these are sprinkled around the environment whenever the cat scratches. From two days to three weeks later, the eggs hatch into gray maggot-like larvae. The larvae hide from the light and feed on organic debris such as crumbs in the carpet. The larvae spin cocoons and emerge as adult fleas. Fleas may live up to four months without feeding; they are not host-specific and will bite a variety of animals, including humans.

An infested cat becomes restless, loses condition, and spoils its coat by constant biting and scratching. Some cats develop an allergy to flea bites that results in a skin condition known as "flea allergy dermatitis." Control of fleas involves a variety of techniques, including bathing, using flea combs, powdering, dipping (best on-the-cat protection), insecticidal bombing of the house, and providing flea tags and collars. Flea combs, which have closely spaced teeth, can be used to remove the parasites from a cat. The fleas should then be transferred to a container of soapy water where they will drown. Currently there is no way to kill flea eggs, so new hatchings constantly must be battled.

Many insecticides which are safe for dogs are *toxic* to cats. Be sure to read the label of the product you purchase to see if it can be used on cats and kittens. Flea tags and collars should be aired for 24 hours before placing them on your Abyssinian. When placing the collar on your Aby, allow enough room for two fingers to fit underneath the collar to ensure proper fit. Some animals are sensitive to flea collars and develop irritation

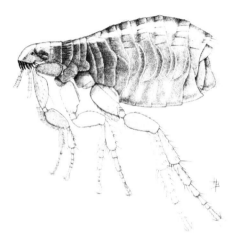

Fleas are a nuisance, especially to cats and dogs, and they are difficult to get rid of. Besides being annoying pests themselves (they can irritate your cat's skin and cause unrelentless itching until the cat ruins its beautiful coat from continuous biting and scratching), fleas are also carriers of such parasites as tapeworms.

of the skin surrounding the neck; if this occurs, remove the collar immediately and use another method of flea control. It should be noted that in heavily infested areas, several control measures must be used together and on a regular basis in order to eliminate this parasite.

Ticks

Ticks are not commonly found on cats; however, it is possible for a cat to become infested. These insects burrow with their heads into the skin, where they suck blood. Sprays and powders specifically designed for cats are effective.

Ear Mites

These microscopic spider-relatives live in the cat's ear canals where they feed on wax and debris. Irritation of the skin that lines the ear canals produces head shaking and loss of hair behind the ears due to scratching. The ears will appear dirty with dark brown granular material. Secondary bacterial infection may occur. Occasionally, when left untreated, the infestation may cause internal ear infections.

Treatment involves cleaning the ears to remove the accumulated debris and using one of several commercially available compounds which contain an insecticide to kill the mites. It is important to follow your veterinarian's instructions completely when using these products and to continue treatment for at least three weeks. There is no way to kill the eggs; thus, treatment must be continued long enough to allow all the eggs to hatch.

Ringworm

This is not really a disease caused by a worm, but rather a fungal disease which may be transmitted to humans. There are several species of ringworm. The mold lives in areas such as the hair and skin; it does not cause infection internally, but it is unsightly and presents a public health problem.

The infection usually starts on the areas of the body which are sparsely haired, such as around the eyes, ears, and feet. Typically, these affected areas have gray, flaky patches of skin with balding and numerous broken-off hairs. The fungus occurs naturally in the soil and it may be spread by carrier cats. Prompt attention is necessary to prevent the infection from spreading to other areas of the body.

Diagnosis is made by the use of fungal cultures, microscopic examination of the hair and skin, and the use of the Wood's lamp. The Wood's lamp is an ultraviolet light source which is held over the suspect lesion. A few species of ringworm will glow under ultraviolet light.

Treatment consists of medicated baths, as well as surface and oral antifungal agents. Treatment often needs to be continued for several weeks.

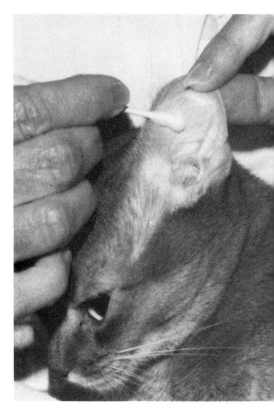

If ever there appears a dark brown granular material in your cat's ears, suspect the presence of ear mites. **Above:** Your veterinarian can show you how to properly clean the cat's ears (which should be done regularly, ear mites or not), and he or she will probably suggest an effective ear mite remedy (**below**).

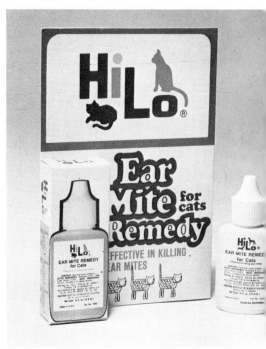

Nutrition

by Kate Faler and Kenna L. Mawk, D.V.M.

Good nutrition is essential for the continued health of your Abyssinian. The task of providing a nutritionally adequate diet is not as difficult as it once was. Pet food companies have flooded the market with a variety of nutritious, tasty, convenient, and appealing foods. It makes sense to base your cat's diet on one of these products.

In 1969, the Federal Trade Commission set guidelines for the pet food industry. They required that any food labeled "complete and balanced," "nutritional," "scientific," or "adequate" must be able to support an animal at any stage of the life cycle when fed as the only food. These foods must meet the requirements set by the National Research Council (NRC) of the National Academy of Sciences, which periodically designates minimum daily requirements for many animal species, including humans.

Nutritional Requirements for Cats

The basic nutrients required to sustain life are protein, carbohydrates, fats, water, vitamins, and minerals.

Protein. This nutrient is required by the body to construct and repair cells and tissues, to build immunity, to synthesize hormones necessary for regulation of body functions, and for the production of enzymes necessary to metabolize food.

Protein is composed of smaller chemical units called amino acids. Some amino acids are referred to as "essential," as they cannot be synthesized in the body but must be supplied in the diet.

Many other animals, such as humans, utilize carbohydrates for energy, but cats burn protein as their main energy source. Feline protein requirements, for example, are twice those of dogs; for this reason, dog food is not adequate for cats.

Dry food should contain at least 21% protein in order to meet the needs of adult cats and should contain at least 33% protein for kittens. Canned or moist foods should contain at least 6% protein for cats and 10% for kittens.

The quality of protein is important. Quality is determined by the types and relative amounts of amino acids present in the protein source. Animal products such as meats, fish, and poultry are the best sources but should be cooked and varied in the diet. Eggs constitute the highest quality of protein available; however, eggs should be cooked or the white should be separated out, as raw egg white contains a substance which binds biotin, a B vitamin, and thus prevents its utilization by the animal. Milk is a good source of protein, but it is not a nutritionally adequate diet alone.

Fats. The actual fat requirement for cats is low; however, the diet can contain quite a high level without causing problems. The usual fat content of the diet is 15 to 40% of the dry weight. Fats contribute to the taste appeal of the food and supply energy. They are necessary for absorption of certain vitamins.

Fats are made up of groups of smaller units called fatty acids. Essential fatty acids are those which must be supplied in the diet. The cat has a particular need for arachadinic acid, which is manufactured in the body by most other animals. Fortunately, this is supplied by most animal fats.

Rancid or oxidized unsaturated fatty acids can lead to the disease called steatitis or "yellow fat disease." This is an inflammation of the fatty tissues and was once a problem in cats fed large amounts of red tuna fish and foods high in fish oils. Manufacturers now add antioxidants, such as Vitamin E, to these types of foods.

Carbohydrates. Cats do not have a requirement for carbohydrates, but these can be utilized by the body if cooked. The addition of rice, potatoes, and bread will add variety to the cat's diet and may comprise as much as 50% of the dry weight. These foods supply complex carbohydrates or starch. Many cats do not tolerate simple carbohydrates, or sugars, such as sucrose or lactose. Adult cats, in particular, may develop diarrhea from cow's milk due to the fermentation of lactose in their intestines.

Water. All animals should have unlimited access to clean, fresh water. Cats on a strictly dry food diet may consume up to ten times the amount of water they would when eating canned foods.

Vitamins. Deficiency of vitamins may lead to a variety of conditions. A well-balanced diet does not usually need added vitamins. Deficiencies may occur when a cat is fed solely one food or on dry food that has been stored for a long period of time or has been improperly processed.

Vitamins are divided into two groups. Fat-soluble vitamins include A, D, E, and K and may be stored in the body. Fat must be present in the diet in order for the fat-soluble vitamins to be absorbed from the intestine. The B-complex vitamins and vitamin C are water-soluble and are not stored.

Vitamin C is not needed in the cat's diet, as the body manufactures this daily requirement. Many of the B-complex vitamins are supplied in animal products or are manufactured by intestinal bacteria.

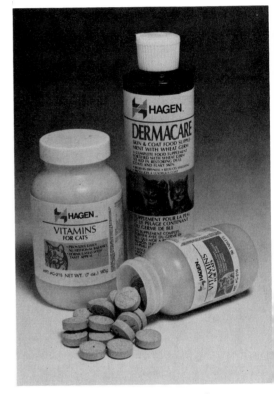

Cats need a well-balanced diet of proteins, carbohydrates, fats, vitamins, minerals, and water in order to maintain good health. Vitamin supplements can be offered to help keep your cat's diet nutritionally complete.

Vitamin B₁ or thiamine deficiency is sometimes seen in cats fed exclusively on one diet over a long period of time. Also, some types of fish contain an enzyme called thiaminase which destroys this vitamin. Thiaminase is inactivated by heat; therefore, only cooked fish should be fed.

Most animals are capable of forming vitamin A from its precursor, beta-carotene, which is present in many orange or yellow plant sources such as carrots; however, cats cannot manufacture their own vitamin A and must have fully formed vitamin A supplied in their diet. Also, cats have an unusually high requirement for vitamin A. Overdosing of this vitamin can be as harmful as underdosing. Vitamin A toxicosis has been seen in cats fed a diet high in liver. Liver is an excellent source of vitamin A; however, it should not be fed more than two or three times a week.

Vitamin D is manufactured in the skin from sunlight, and vitamin K is synthesized by intestinal bacteria as well as being supplied by liver and soybean meal. Vitamin E deficiency is manifested as steatitis and occurs when cats are fed a diet consisting mainly of canned tuna fish or a diet high in unsaturated fats.

Minerals. Calcium is required in high amounts, especially during lactation and growth. It is used in conjunction with phosphorus by the cat's body (the ideal ratio of calcium to phosphorus should be 1:1). Red meat diets are high in phosphorus, in proportion to their calcium content, and should not be fed exclusively because they cause an upset of this balance, resulting in calcium deficiency. Vitamin D is necessary for the proper utilization of calcium and phosphorus.

Iron, along with copper, is needed for blood formation. Other necessary minerals that are needed in the cat's diet are cobalt, sodium, chlorine, potassium, iodine, magnesium, and zinc.

Types of Diets

As kittens, Abyssinians must be exposed to a variety of foods. If fed a single food, they will not find others acceptable when they become adults. Table scraps are fine for a treat, but they should not be substituted for a balanced diet. Cats are like people in that they will develop individual likes and dislikes. They will not become "finicky" eaters unless they expect that they will be fed only their favorite food.

Commercial foods manufactured by well-known companies are usually backed by a great deal of research. Most commercial foods are formulated to be complete diets; thus, it is best to base your Abyssinian's diet on a variety of these foods.

Most of the varieties are an adequate diet for growth and maintenance; however, they may not meet the needs for reproduction and lactation. Be sure to check the label for feeding recommendations for growth, reproduction, and lactation. If feeding recommendations are not given for these stages of development, then assume it is not adequate for those needs and either supplement the diet or use a different ration.

Commercial foods fall into three basic groups:

Dry Foods. These are excellent snack foods with a long storage life. An average food will contain 30% protein, 7% fat, and 9-10% moisture. They help clean the teeth and massage the gums to reduce the incidence of gingivitis. If you are going to be away for a weekend, they make an excellent self-feeding system. Dry foods are composed primarily of a grain base mixed with a variety of meat by-product meals.

Dry food is not as palatable as other forms unless the cat is accustomed to it. Dry food is not recommended as the only food in the cat's diet, as it usually does not contain the protein of canned food and the cat may not find it tasty enough to eat a sufficient amount to supply its daily requirements. Moistening the food or mixing it with canned food eliminates the benefits of teeth and gum exercise.

Many veterinarians feel that the high ash content of dry food contributes to the feline urologic syndrome (FUS). There have been some studies conducted which may support this theory (Oliphant and Tovey, 1977). Those cats who are prone to FUS probably should not be fed dry food.

Canned Foods. Canned food must, by definition, contain more moisture than dry food. It may contain as much as 75% water; thus, you are paying for less actual food value. Water content and texture should be considered, as they influence palatability as much as flavor does. Many canned foods are designed to appeal to owners rather than to cats.

There are two major types of canned food. The small-sized cans (usually six ounces) are higher in protein and fat and may contain up to 95% meat. In general, they are not designed as a complete diet, but rather as a highly flavored protein supplement. An average can might contain 10-23% protein, 2-6% fat, and 75% moisture. Labels like "meat flavor" and "dinner" may indicate less meat.

Usually the regular rations are sold in larger cans and contain 12 to 15 ounces. These contain about 10% protein, 2% fat, and 75% moisture. Typically, these foods contain a fairly high amount of cereal grains.

One advantage of canned food is that the nutritional value is not affected by storage. Disadvantages are that canned food is more expensive, cannot be self-fed, (it spoils if left out), and some of the specialty foods sold in the smaller cans may not be nutritionally complete.

Soft-moist. These foods were designed to fill the gap between dry foods and canned foods. They are convenient, keep well, and do not have the strong odor of canned food; additionally, they are more tasty than dry food. On the other hand, many experts object to the high carbohydrate and preservative levels. Normally, they contain at least 27% protein, 7% fat, and 32% moisture.

Home Diets. It is not economical to mix your own cat food diet from the basic ingredients unless you have a number of cats. In addition, it requires quite a bit of time and knowledge of nutritional principles to create a balanced diet in this way. Two home diets that are known to be nutritionally adequate are given here (Collins, 1976).

D'Arcy Cattery Diet

4 lbs. raw hamburger
1/2 lb. raw liver, ground
2 lbs. Purina Hi-Protein Dog Meal
1/4 lb. Theralin vitamins (8 tbsp.)
1/4 lb. brewer's yeast (10 tbsp.)

Soak dog food in enough hot water to cover. Mix in hamburger, liver, and dry ingredients (theralin, yeast). If mixture is too dry, add a little water. If too soupy, add Gerber's Baby Rice Cereal. Should be fed at the rate of 1/2 ounce per pound of cat.

National Research Council's Diet A (modified)

1 lb. cottage cheese
1/2 lb. whole dried milk
3/4 lb. raw liver
3 cups oatmeal (uncooked)
1 1/2 ozs. brewer's yeast (6¼ tbsp.)
3/4 oz. cod liver oil

Mix cod liver oil with cottage cheese and liver (ground or blended). Mix in milk and brewer's yeast. Finally, fold in oatmeal, adding a little water if needed for a smooth blend.

Feeding Regimen

Cats should be fed twice a day, but dry snack foods can be left out for nibbling. Environmental factors influencing eating habits may include the cleanliness of the food dishes, the presence or absence of people or other animals, light, and noise. If your cat is not eating, careful observation during the cat's meal time will allow you to detect interfering stimuli.

Occasionally, supplement the cat's diet with raw egg yolk or cooked egg, cheese, yogurt, large uncooked beef bones to chew, meat-type baby food, cooked meat, cooked fish, and vegetables. Avoid giving poultry bones, pork bones, or small beef bones. Poultry bones are hollow and splinter easily into sharp spikes; small cooked beef and pork bones also will fragment in this manner and could be dangerous to your cat.

When cats that are conditioned to eat one type of food are switched to another type, be patient during this transition period. Continue to offer the new food at meal time; if your cat refuses it, do not offer it again until the next meal. During this time, remove all dry food. As the cat becomes hungry enough, it will eat the new food. Sometimes a new food may be introduced by adding small amounts to the current diet, then gradually increasing the proportion of the new ingredient.

Meal time is a big event for Abys. They enjoy their food, but it is up to you to provide a balanced diet for them. Good health depends more upon proper nutrition than on any other single factor. Abyssinians seldom become overweight, and as a rule of thumb, you can feed them all they will eat. When you cannot feel the cat's ribs, then it is time to cut down on the portions.

NUTRITIONAL REQUIREMENTS

Protein and Energy Requirements of Cats +

	Req. * in	Req. * * Per Cat	
	Food	Kitten (10 wks.)	Adult
Protein (%)	30	8.6	2.9
Energy (Cal./100g.)	400	115.0	40.0

+ Modified from NRC (1978)
 * Expressed on a DM basis (DM = dry matter, determined by weight after the water has been removed by drying for long periods in an oven).
* * Expressed as amts./lb. body weight/day.

Vitamin Requirements of Cats +

	Req. * in	Req. * * Per Cat	
Vitamin	Food	Kitten (10 wks.)	Adult
A (IU)	1000.0	290.00	100.00
D (IU)	100.0	29.00	10.00
E (IU)	10.0	3.00	1.00
Thiamin (mg.)	0.5	0.14	0.05
Riboflavin (mg.)	0.5	0.14	0.05
PA (mg.)	1.0	0.28	0.10
Niacin (mg.)	4.5	1.00	0.50
Pyridoxine (microg.)	400.0	140.00	45.00
Folic Acid (microg.)	100.0	30.00	9.00
Biotin (microg.)	5.0	1.00	0.50
B_{12} (microg.)	2.0	0.60	0.20
Choline (mg.)	200.0	57.00	20.00

+ Modified from NRC (1978)
* Expressed as amts. per 100 g. food DM.
* * Expressed as amts./lb. body weight/day.

Mineral Requirements of Cats +

1. Macro-minerals

Mineral	Req. in * Food	Req. ** Per Cat Kitten (10 wks.)	Adult
Calcium	1000	290	90
Phosphorus	800	230	80
Magnesium	50	14	5
Potassium	300	90	30
Salt (Nacl)	500	140	50

\+ Modified from NRC (1978)
* Expressed as mg./100 g. food DM
** Expressed as mg./lb. body weight/day.

2. Micro-minerals

Mineral	Req. in * Food	Req. ** Per Cat Kitten (10 wks.)	Adult
Iron	100.0	30.00	10.000
Copper	5.0	1.40	0.500
Manganese	10.0	2.80	0.900
Zinc	30.0	8.60	3.200
Iodine	1.0	0.30	0.090
Selenium	0.1	0.03	0.009

\+ Modified from NRC (1978)
* Expressed as ppm DM.
** Expressed as microgram/lb. body weight/day.

This healthy Aby has a special glow that reflects good care. Besides well-balanced meals, exercise, and lots of loving human contact, cats need some grooming attention as well; however, since Abyssinians are shorthaired, grooming need not be complicated.

Grooming Your Abyssinian

by Kim Everett

The Bath

The best method of bathing your Aby is to first fill the bathtub or sink up to about where the cat's chest level would be. Turn off the water before fetching the cat, as it is the sound of running water that frightens many Abys. The water should be comfortably warm. Remember, the cat's normal body temperature is slightly higher than yours. Hold your Abyssinian (as described earlier) by placing one hand under its rib cage while supporting its body with the other hand under its rear paws. Now, lower the cat gently into the water. Talk softly and reassuringly to your cat. It is recommended that you begin bathing your kitten at about five months old to get it accustomed to the process; however, a cat of any age need not be difficult to bathe using this technique.

Choose a mild protein shampoo and never a detergent-type that dries out the coat. You may use shampoos made for redheads if they *do not* contain any artificial coloring. Such coloring can be hazardous to the health of your cat. If you have an Aby with a tight, sleek coat and you want to add body, there are good protein body-building shampoos. Obviously, if your Aby has a good resilient coat, do not overdo it with body building shampoos or conditioners or your cat will look like a porcupine. Diluting the shampoo 50% with water and sponging it on will allow even distribution of the suds and less waste.

After applying the shampoo, lather your Aby up to the neck, cheeks, and top of its head. Wash the cat's face with a damp wash cloth to avoid getting shampoo in the eyes. Abys, especially males, tend to become very oily around the tail and neck, so they may need a second shampoo in these areas. Rinse the cat well with warm water and be certain to get all the shampoo out to prevent irritation of the skin due to soap residue.

The next step will be a final rinse with one quart of warm water containing a tablespoon of cider vinegar. This will do wonders for the coat by adding shine and body as well as by cutting down shedding, because it removes the soap. Gently take your Aby out of the tub, and with a large absorbent towel blot all the excess water out of the coat. The cat may help you in the drying process by licking and shaking itself.

You will want to purchase a fine-toothed steel grooming comb (Belgian combs are the best). Comb in the direction of the coat to remove dead hair. Start at the head and work to the tail. Be sure not to miss the undersides, including from the chin down, chest, belly, and pants.

An ideal time to apply a coat conditioner is when the Aby is damp-dry. Again, there are many good products on the market. (I feel conditioners that do not need to be washed out are best.) Use the conditioner sparingly by moistening the palms of your hands and working them through the coat. Next, comb it through with the comb. Finally, use a hair dryer and continue to comb with the grain of the coat until it is thoroughly dry. (I have found that turning the dryer to "high" causes less excitement than the low setting. Perhaps it is the lower frequency sound which disturbs some cats.) Experiment with the dryer speed your Aby finds most comfortable. By this time your Aby should literally "glow" and be as proud as a peacock.

The Ears

You may want to clean your Aby's ears with cotton-tipped swabs moistened in a bit of baby oil. Do not clean down into the ear canal, as this could remove the protective ear wax which helps prevent infections. Now is an ideal time to check your Aby for any signs of ear mites or infections of the ear. (See the External Parasites section.)

If you are showing your Aby, and it has excessive hair in its ears (this does not include the lovely tufts at the tips that some Abyssinians have), use a small pair of cuticle scissors to clip this excess hair out. Do not shave the inside of the ear, as a natural appearance which reflects good grooming is desired. There still should be a fine layer of hair remaining in the ear. The effect you want to achieve is ears that look as large as possible and that are "clean" and open at the base.

The Final Touch

Never use a rubber comb or chamois on your Aby. This will ruin the beautiful coat for which Abyssinians are known. The Aby has resilient hair, not close-lying and sleek hair like the Siamese or Burmese (a chamois works beautifully for them).

If you are going to show your Aby, pack a grooming kit with cotton-tipped swabs, claw clippers, and a fine-toothed comb. At the show, you need only to "hand groom" your Aby by rubbing its coat from head to tail with the natural lie of the hair. Since your hands contain natural oils, these will enhance the Aby's coat as you hand groom. (Incidentally, this can be

Show cats should be bathed a few days prior to the big event. Pet shops stock mild shampoos that are safe to use on cats.

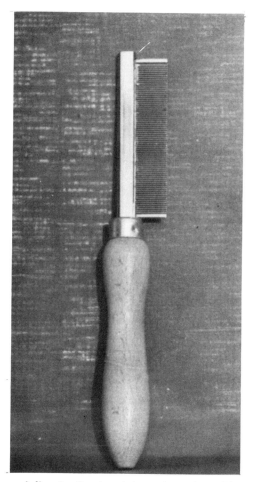

A fine-toothed metal comb such as this (32 teeth per inch) is a necessary part of your Aby's grooming kit. Such a comb will help remove loose hairs from the cat's coat and will also catch any fleas that may be lurking amidst the hairs.

A soft-bristled brush is an optional piece of equipment to keep in the grooming kit. Never use a firm or rubber-tined brush.

done anytime, not just for a show.) You may wish to use a silk scarf for a final polish just before the cat enters the judging ring, but remember, the important aspects of grooming are bathing, claw clipping, and ear cleaning, all of which should be done prior to the show. A bath three to four days in advance of the show is best, as it allows the Aby's coat to regain the natural oils which give it body.

The Color

Males generally retain their coat color, but it is common for females to lighten or darken according to their heat cycle. This is natural, so do not become alarmed if it occurs.

Maintaining your Aby's best color involves good grooming, proper diet, love, exercise, and plenty of sun and ventilation. Abys will not do well in small confined quarters away from light and attention. They require the constant companionship and love of their family and other pets.

Abys are "people" cats, and with proper care you will be well rewarded for your efforts.

Selective breeding of cats requires a knowledge of
genetics, pedigrees, and the breed standard.

Breeding Abyssinians

Breeding cats is an art as well as a science, and it should be practiced only by those serious cat fanciers who have the time, money, knowledge and experience to develop sound breeding programs. The selection of breeding stock determines the rate of improvement or decline in a cattery. Careful study of pedigrees, winning cats, and the breed standard is necessary before the best decisions can be made. Sometimes a breeder will play a hunch or just have a feeling that a particular combination will work; other times the decision is based on an in-depth study of many generations of cats. In addition, a truly top breeding program involves a systematic upgrading of stock. It is hoped that the offspring will be better than either of its parents. Thus, a periodic cold-hearted evaluation of all Abys in a cattery must be made and those that are no longer of value with regard to improving the breed should be altered and placed in other homes as pets. This is a hard task and an especially difficult one, thanks to the endearing, unique personality traits of each Abyssinian. However, if this is not done, a cattery becomes overburdened with neutered pets or with now-mediocre queens and studs that have lost those dynamic qualities necessary to produce winning cats. Daily chores to keep these cats become greater and greater, while the rewards are fewer and fewer. The result is that a cattery name becomes known for producing pet-quality kittens but rarely outstanding show specimens; additionally, overcrowding rapidly leads to health problems.

The best approach to selective breeding is to realize from the beginning that only a few high-quality cats (I suggest no more than ten, but five is better if you are working) will be kept. Give them lots of love and care while they live in the cattery, and eventually place them in loving homes where they will be cherished as important members of the family for years to come. (See the Genetics section, under the heading "Selection.")

Abyssinians reach puberty at a later age than most other breeds. Wait until the cats are at least one year of age before breeding them to ensure that nutrients normally used for their own growth will not be diverted for reproduction. After selecting the combination of sire and dam, it is necessary to make sure they are in the best of health.

The Estrous Cycle

Male cats are capable of mating year-round, but females have periodic cycles that may last from ten to 14 days. The eggs ripen in a fluid-filled sac, called a follicle, on the ovaries. The cells surrounding the follicle produce the hormone estrogen that is responsible for the visible signs of "heat" or estrous in female cats. Most people find it easy to detect heat in female cats, as the signs involve calling, rolling, rubbing, crouching on the stomach, treading with the hind feet, spraying urine, restlessness, and loss of appetite. The eggs are only ovulated or released under the stimulus of mating, due to the barbs on the male cat's penis which stimulate the vagina. If mating does not occur, the follicles regress and the cycle repeats itself every two to three weeks. When mating does occur, the cycle is shortened. Some believe that this cycle is nature's way of ensuring reproduction by normally solitary felines. Female pack or herd animals are likely to have mates available, but female cats hunt alone and need to be receptive if and when a male cat is present. Some queens (unaltered female cats) will go through a quiet period with no cycling around the month of January. The length of the day cues a female cat that if she were to become pregnant, the kittens would be born in the winter when conditions are adverse. Artificial lighting has altered this age-old pattern, and most queens (especially those kept indoors) cycle all year long. Both males and females may be fertile throughout their lifetimes.

It is a good idea to record heat periods for each female cat. Eventually, a pattern will become evident that will be helpful when predicting breeding dates.

Stud Service For Your Queen

If possible, select a local tom (unaltered male cat) for breeding. This will allow you to inspect the cattery and discuss the details in person, rather than over the telephone or through the mail. Arrangements should be made well in advance of the actual date of the mating. When a queen is sexually receptive, i.e., when she is ready to receive the male, normally she is sent to the male's owner, as some males will not breed unless they are in their own territory. The two are introduced through a door or cage and are allowed to gradually become familiar with each other. Usually they will begin an extended conversation of soft trills when they are ready to be placed together. The owner of the stud should witness all the breedings. Usually, the pair is let in together on two or three separate occasions during the day. Breedings usually are not allowed after 48 hours, in order to accurately judge the arrival date of the kittens. Females should be bred about the third day of a strong heat. If a female is being shipped to a male (and this usually is the case with serious breeders), she will need more time to adjust, so she is best sent at the first signs of estrous.

Courtship behavior varies from cat to cat and may take minutes to days, but the actual mating takes very little time. The tom holds on to the queen by the back of her neck and mounts her. Erection and ejaculation occur almost immediately. The queen cries out, rolls, and may turn on the male. Both cats lick their genital areas afterwards.

Some breeders like to keep virgin queens until pregnancy is confirmed, but proven queens are usually returned to their owners as soon as possible. Ideally, inexperienced cats of either sex should be bred first with an experienced mate in order to assure that the mating proceeds smoothly.

Gestation

The first signs of pregnancy may be morning sickness, decreased activity, and enlarging of the nipples, which become darker pink in color. Three weeks after breeding, an experienced person can detect the changes in the feel of the queen's uterus. Some pregnant queens will have a second heat halfway through gestation, and if they are allowed to breed, this may result in kittens of different ages, the youngest of which are premature when born. Normal gestation is 63 to 65 days but ranges from 58 to 71 days.

The queen will gradually increase her consumption of food, and it is best to let her eat all she wants. In the last trimester of pregnancy, it is a good idea to supplement her regular diet with extra protein (meat, poultry, fish, eggs, or cheese) and calcium. Calcium always should be supplied in a two-to-one ratio with phosphorus (for pregnant queens). Activity level will slowly decrease as the queen increases in size, and she should be protected from high places. Mammary development will increase late in pregnancy, and when the queen is at rest, movement of the kittens can be felt.

The queen will begin to look for a suitable nesting place. This is the time to decide on a mutually acceptable location, because once an Aby makes up its mind, it becomes very difficult to change it. She will want an area that is quiet, sheltered, dry, dim, and isolated from other animals. A spot that is accessible and easy to clean is important.

A kittening box can be constructed from a large cardboard box. Be sure to design it so that it is covered on the top (with a removable lid, so that you can check on the new family from time to time) and has a door for exit that is elevated from the box floor level so the kittens will not fall out. The box should be raised off the floor for warmth and protection from drafts. A heating pad with a low setting may be added for cold nights or small litters that do not generate enough body heat to keep warm when the mother is away from the box. Line the box with soft material such as old sheets or disposable diapers.

KITTENING CHART

	JANUARY																															
Mated	01	02	03	04	05	06	07	08	09	10	11	12	13	14	15	16	17	18	19	20	21	22	23	24	25	26	27	28	29	30	31
Kittens	7	8	9	10	11	12	13	14	15	16	17	18	19	20	21	22	23	24	25	26	27	28	29	30	31	01	02	03	04	05	06
	MARCH																										APRIL				

	FEBRUARY																											
Mated	01	02	03	04	05	06	07	08	09	10	11	12	13	14	15	16	17	18	19	20	21	22	23	24	25	26	27	28
Kittens	7	8	9	10	11	12	13	14	15	16	17	18	19	20	21	22	23	24	25	26	27	28	29	30	01	02	03	04
	APRIL																								MAY			

	MARCH																														
Mated	01	02	03	04	05	06	07	08	09	10	11	12	13	14	15	16	17	18	19	20	21	22	23	24	25	26	27	28	29	30	31
Kittens	5	6	7	8	9	10	11	12	13	14	15	16	17	18	19	20	21	22	23	24	25	26	27	28	29	30	31	01	02	03	04
	MAY																										JUNE			

	APRIL																													
Mated	01	02	03	04	05	06	07	08	09	10	11	12	13	14	15	16	17	18	19	20	21	22	23	24	25	26	27	28	29	30
Kittens	5	6	7	8	9	10	11	12	13	14	15	16	17	18	19	20	21	22	23	24	25	26	27	28	29	30	01	02	03	04
	JUNE																									JULY			

	MAY																														
Mated	01	02	03	04	05	06	07	08	09	10	11	12	13	14	15	16	17	18	19	20	21	22	23	24	25	26	27	28	29	30	31
Kittens	5	6	7	8	9	10	11	12	13	14	15	16	17	18	19	20	21	22	23	24	25	26	27	28	29	30	31	01	02	03	04
	JULY																										AUGUST			

	JUNE																													
Mated	01	02	03	04	05	06	07	08	09	10	11	12	13	14	15	16	17	18	19	20	21	22	23	24	25	26	27	28	29	30
Kittens	5	6	7	8	9	10	11	12	13	14	15	16	17	18	19	20	21	22	23	24	25	26	27	28	29	30	31	01	02	03
	AUGUST																								SEPTEMBER			

	JULY																														
Mated	01	02	03	04	05	06	07	08	09	10	11	12	13	14	15	16	17	18	19	20	21	22	23	24	25	26	27	28	29	30	31
Kittens	4	5	6	7	8	9	10	11	12	13	14	15	16	17	18	19	20	21	22	23	24	25	26	27	28	29	30	01	02	03	04
	SEPTEMBER																								OCTOBER			

	AUGUST																														
Mated	01	02	03	04	05	06	07	08	09	10	11	12	13	14	15	16	17	18	19	20	21	22	23	24	25	26	27	28	29	30	31
Kittens	5	6	7	8	9	10	11	12	13	14	15	16	17	18	19	20	21	22	23	24	25	26	27	28	29	30	31	01	02	03	04
	OCTOBER																								NOVEMBER			

	SEPTEMBER																													
Mated	01	02	03	04	05	06	07	08	09	10	11	12	13	14	15	16	17	18	19	20	21	22	23	24	25	26	27	28	29	30
Kittens	5	6	7	8	9	10	11	12	13	14	15	16	17	18	19	20	21	22	23	24	25	26	27	28	29	30	01	02	03	04
	NOVEMBER																								DECEMBER			

	OCTOBER																														
Mated	01	02	03	04	05	06	07	08	09	10	11	12	13	14	15	16	17	18	19	20	21	22	23	24	25	26	27	28	29	30	31
Kittens	5	6	7	8	9	10	11	12	13	14	15	16	17	18	19	20	21	22	23	24	25	26	27	28	29	30	31	01	02	03	04
	DECEMBER																								JANUARY			

	NOVEMBER																													
Mated	01	02	03	04	05	06	07	08	09	10	11	12	13	14	15	16	17	18	19	20	21	22	23	24	25	26	27	28	29	30
Kittens	5	6	7	8	9	10	11	12	13	14	15	16	17	18	19	20	21	22	23	24	25	26	27	28	29	30	31	01	02	03
	JANUARY																								FEBRUARY			

	DECEMBER																														
Mated	01	02	03	04	05	06	07	08	09	10	11	12	13	14	15	16	17	18	19	20	21	22	23	24	25	26	27	28	29	30	31
Kittens	4	5	6	7	8	9	10	11	12	13	14	15	16	17	18	19	20	21	22	23	24	25	26	27	28	01	02	03	04	05	06
	FEBRUARY																								MARCH			

An Aby queen with her four-day-old litter of three. For the first few days, do not disturb the queen and her kittens, except to offer the mother food and water.

Opposite:
By locating the date a female cat was mated (top line), one can determine the birthdate (bottom line) of the kittens. This chart is based on a 65-day gestation period.

(Terrycloth towels *are not* satisfactory, as young kittens are incapable of retracting their claws which easily become snagged on the rough surface.) The queen, incidentally, will rearrange the bedding to her satisfaction. Do not interfere as the queen prepares her nest.

As the big day approaches, carefully clip the hair around the queen's nipples with a pair of blunt-end scissors. This will help the newborn kittens locate their meals. Assemble scissors, paper towels, iodine, forceps, a notebook, a pencil, and disinfectant for your hands. A small inexpensive postage/diet type of scale should be purchased for weighing the kittens.

Parturition

A few days before the kittens are due, the mother's milk will be present in her mammary glands. To check the milk supply, gently squeeze a teat with a downward motion. It is important to repeat this after the kittens are born to make sure milk is flowing in the nipples.

The queen usually will let you know when the birth is pending. She will make frequent changes in the arrangement of the bedding in her nest. Pacing, crying, and increasing her demand for human attention also communicate the fact. Someone knowledgeable, with breeding experience, should be present. Do not just "let nature takes its course," as during parturition most queens need help from time to time. A decrease in body temperature to 99° - 100°F. occurs in some, but not all, queens 12-24 hours before the birth.

The next "clue" that parturition is imminent is when the queen stays in her nesting box and refuses to leave. In a little while, hard contractions begin. She will sit in a crouched position or on her chest, and with each contraction, her abdomen compresses, her whiskers tilt forward, and she stretches out her hind legs. She may turn about and lick her vulva. Panting and crying occur.

As each kitten is born, it is surrounded with a fluid-filled sac which usually ruptures. If the sac does not break, the mother will tear it off as she licks the kitten. Be prepared to remove each sac if the queen will not; otherwise, the kittens will drown in the fluid. Once each kitten is detached from the womb, the oxygen supply is cut off, so it is important that the kittens be born as rapidly as possible. Should you be able to see part of the kitten but the mother cannot push it out, take a cloth for traction and gently pull down and out on the kitten during the mother's contractions. Incidentally, breech births, in which the kitten is born hind end first, occur normally about 50% of the time.

The newborn kitten still will be attached to the placenta (afterbirth) by the umbilical cord, and normally the mother will chew the cord off. If she does not, or if the kitten is in need of attention and the placenta has not yet been delivered, tear the umbilical cord or cut it with sterilized scissors or a sterilized dull

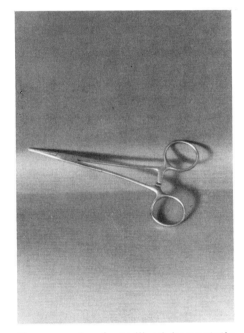

Keep a pair of sterilized hemostatic forceps on hand in case during parturition you need to cut a kitten's umbilical cord. Normally the queen will take care of this by chewing the cord, but if she fails to do so, you must intervene.

After several contractions, the newborn kitten emerges. The queen stimulates the kitten's breathing by licking off remnants of amniotic fluid from the face.

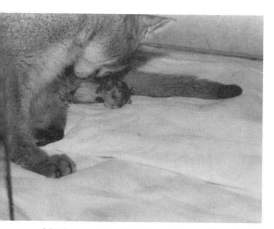

Mother cat's licking also stimulates the kitten's circulation. After the kitten has fully emerged and its umbilical cord has been severed, it should be followed by its placenta (birth sac).

A contented queen purrs while her kit, who is only ten minutes old, finds nourishment.

knife, using a sawing motion. Actually, the best method is to first clamp the cord with hemostatic forceps, since a sharp cut will not crush the vessel closed and can allow stressful bleeding to occur. If bleeding does occur, apply direct pressure by pinching the end of the cord in your fingers for a few minutes. (Remember, this cord carried a large part of the kitten's circulation; thus, it is a large vessel with access to a large volume of blood.) It is better to cut the cord too long than too short. When cutting the cord, do not pull on the side that is attached to the kitten's abdomen, as an umbilical hernia may result. Dipping the cut end of the cord in tincture of iodine will help to prevent infections. As the kitten gets older, the stump will dry up and fall off.

It is important to quickly remove any mucus and fluid that may be in the kitten's nose and mouth so it can breathe freely. If, for some reason, the mother does not do this by her rough licking, take the kitten in your hand and gently wipe its face with a paper towel or cloth. If the kitten appears to be choking, a sharp downward swing of the kitten, while holding it firmly in your hands, will force any fluids out. Breathing may be stimulated by vigorously rubbing the kitten or by lightly compressing its chest.

The queen usually will eat each kitten's placenta (or some of them); this is a natural thing for her to do. Keep a record in your notebook so you can be sure all placentas were delivered. Consult your veterinarian if any were retained in the womb, since placentas that are not expelled could cause infection.

Usually there is a rest period between the delivery of each kitten. Use this time to help the newborn kittens find a nipple. Be patient; most newborn Abys seem determined but dense. It is important that all kittens receive the colostrum, or first milk, as it is rich in antibodies which give temporary immunity against disease to the kittens.

When the second kitten appears to be on its way, remove the first kitten to a nearby corner of the nesting box where it will be out of the way but within sight of its mother.

During the whole process, remain calm, speak in a soft voice, allow as few people as possible to witness the birth, and reduce loud noises. The queen should be able to concentrate on the job at hand, with assistance only if necessary. Handle the kittens *carefully* to prevent the high-pitched cries, which seem to distress their mother. A drink of milk or water will be much appreciated by the queen when the event is over.

Consult your veterinarian if any of the following problems occur: if the queen has weak contractions, if the queen has strong contractions but does not produce a kitten within four hours, if she has a bright red vaginal discharge without labor, or if she partially delivers a kitten. It is best to contact the veterinarian first by telephone, as transporting the queen may upset her.

Care of the New Family

For the first few days, the family should be disturbed as little as possible. The queen will appreciate a convenient litter box and food and water dishes. Notes can be taken on the appearance and sex of each kitten; males are identified by the wider distance between the anal and penile openings as compared to the distance between the vulval and anal on the females. In addition, the females' vulval opening appears as a slit rather than a round hole. Many litters are so uniform in appearance that sometimes individual cats must be marked for identification in order to distinguish them among their siblings. Brightly colored, small dots of fingernail polish on the ears seem to work well but occasionally must be replaced.

Each kitten should be weighed daily on the postage/diet scale. (The importance of this routine cannot be stressed enough.) Slow weight gain, no weight gain, or loss in weight often will be your first clue that a kitten is not doing well. Aby kittens usually weigh approximately 100 grams when born. Daily gains should average ten grams. A slow gain in weight may be caused by competition with littermates for food or a low-producing teat. Kittens imprint on a particular nipple soon after birth and will favor and search for that particular one as identified by scent and texture. Kittens that imprint on front teats often do not gain as much as their littermates who have imprinted on the better-producing rear teats. Spend time each day making sure that each kitten gets a fair share of milk. No weight gain for several days or a weight loss is serious. Hydration (see the Health and Safety chapter, Signs of Illness) should be monitored, and perhaps supplemental feedings should be started. This is best accomplished using a stomach tube (not a bottle) as you can be sure an exact amount of formula is getting into the kitten's stomach and is not being spilled. (See the next section, Orphaned or Rejected Kittens, for instructions on how to use a stomach tube.)

The queen grooms one of her six-day-old kittens while it nurses alongside its other littermates. Abyssinians are wonderful mothers.

When the kittens are about ten days old, their eyes will open. It is important to protect their eyes from bright light for a few days until the kittens have adjusted. At this time, clip each of the kitten's claws to prevent the kittens from scratching themselves during a scramble for food. (Kittens are not able to retract their claws.) If possible, one person should hold each kitten while another person trims the claws with a pair of nail clippers. (For kittens, use human nail clippers.) If it is not possible for an assistant to help you, then hold the kitten yourself in one hand and clip the claws with your other hand. Take care not to cut too deeply into the quick (the pink area) or into the paw pad, as this could be very painful to the kitten.

The queen normally will lick each kitten's genital area to stimulate defecation and urination. The waste is then consumed by the mother. If she does not do this, you must use a warm, moist paper towel or cotton ball to rub the anal area gently several times daily, because the kittens will rapidly die without the needed stimulation to expel waste products.

Studies have shown that kittens who are handled frequently, and at a young age, develop faster and show better adjustment than those who are not handled often. (I feel that good pets are a result of systematic conditioning.) Kittens should be held often, talked to, and played with. This is especially important during the time they are being weaned from their mother. If they struggle, do not let them down but continue to pet them. Handling the kittens while they are eating will make them more "people oriented," as they associate the two processes.

A kitten's deciduous or baby teeth erupt during the second or third week of life. The process is pretty much complete by four weeks of age.

Abyssinians make excellent mothers as a general rule, and during the first week or so, many will leave the kittens only if the food, water, and litter box are not placed near the nesting box. Bedding in the box should be changed often. Allow the queen as much regular food as she will eat and supplement her diet with a daily serving of high-quality protein such as meat, eggs, milk, poultry, fish, or cheese. Calcium and phosphorus should be added to the diet to prevent deficiencies. Depending on the number of kittens and their demands, adjust the mother's diet so that she remains in good condition.

Orphaned or Rejected Kittens

In rare cases, a litter of Abyssinian kittens might be orphaned or rejected by their mother. A queen that attacks or refuses her kittens should not be kept within a breeding program.

It is important for the kittens to have the colostrum in the queen's milk, as it will greatly improve their chances for survival. (Antibodies that help build up immunity to disease are passed through the queen's milk.) Even if this involves restraint of the queen, such feeding should be done.

The very best thing to do for rejected kittens is to find a foster mother cat. Cat clubs, newspapers, veterinarians, and so forth are resources available to help you locate one. Time is an important factor, for no kitten formula can totally replace a mother cat's milk. Aby kittens should be allowed to mix with the foster mother's kittens for as long as possible in order to pick up the new scent before returning the foster mother to her nest; however, do not allow the foster mother to become upset or suspicious. Try to match the kittens' ages as closely as possible to prevent unfair competition for food. Any nipples that were not being used will gradually come back into service, if there is a demand for them, but supplementation with additional food for the kittens may be necessary for a few days. Convincing a cat to accept additional kittens is relatively easy, especially if it is not her first litter. (Incidentally, the foster mother first should have been checked for leukemia.)

At three weeks, with eyes fully opened, these three inquisitive kittens are starting to wonder what lies outside their nesting box.

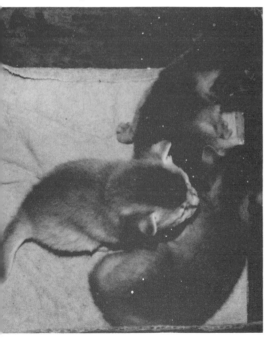

If you decide to raise the kittens yourself, be prepared for a full-time occupation.

Bottle-feeding is one method of hand-raising orphaned or rejected kittens. The nipple of the bottle should have a hole cut in it large enough to drip formula when it is turned upside down. (*Note:* See formula chart at the end of this section.) The bottle should be warmed to cat body temperature (101.5°F.), and the formula should be completely mixed. Place the kitten firmly in your lap (do not place it on its back), hold its head as if you were going to give it a pill, and then introduce the nipple. Do not tilt the kitten's head back. Next, allow a little of the milk to flow out. Do not squeeze the bottle while it is in the kitten's mouth or you may drown the kitten. Be patient; many kittens find a rubber nipple to be a poor substitute for the real thing, especially if they have nursed on their mother before. Once the kitten begins sucking, you will have to gently squeeze the bottle as the level goes down. This feeding procedure should be followed for each abandoned kitten.

Force-feeding with a syringe or eye dropper is another method. Like bottle-feeding, it is also time consuming; however, it is an inaccurate and dangerous method.

The best method involves using a feeding tube to deposit the milk quickly and in a precise amount directly into the kitten's stomach. This is a very easy technique and will save the lives of many kittens who are too weak to nurse. Overall, it is the least dangerous method. It can also be used to feed sick adult cats. The equipment needed is a tiny catheter (#5 or #8 French infant feeding tube) and a syringe. These can be obtained from either your veterinarian or from veterinary supply houses. (Breeders always should keep them on hand.)

The kitten should be held firmly with its mouth opened. The tube is then inserted to a pre-measured length, and the desired amount of milk formula is dispensed with the syringe. The length to insert the feeding tube is determined by the distance from the kitten's nose to the last rib. The possibility of placing the tube in the lungs is the danger most people fear, but it is quite unlikely this will happen. (I know of no one who has lost a kitten this way, and most people who are frightened of it really have little experience with the technique.) Be sure to push all of the air out of the tube before inserting it. Do not withdraw the tube until all the formula has been dispensed. If the kitten is too full, the milk simply will be regurgitated. Each kitten can be fed in this manner.

All feeding equipment should be throughly cleaned and boiled or disinfected and rinsed after each use.

Kitten formulas and a comparison of their ingredients are presented in the following chart. Many breeders have used the home formula successfully; however, KMR or Esbilac (both excellent commercially prepared formulas) are usually available from your veterinarian or pet shop.

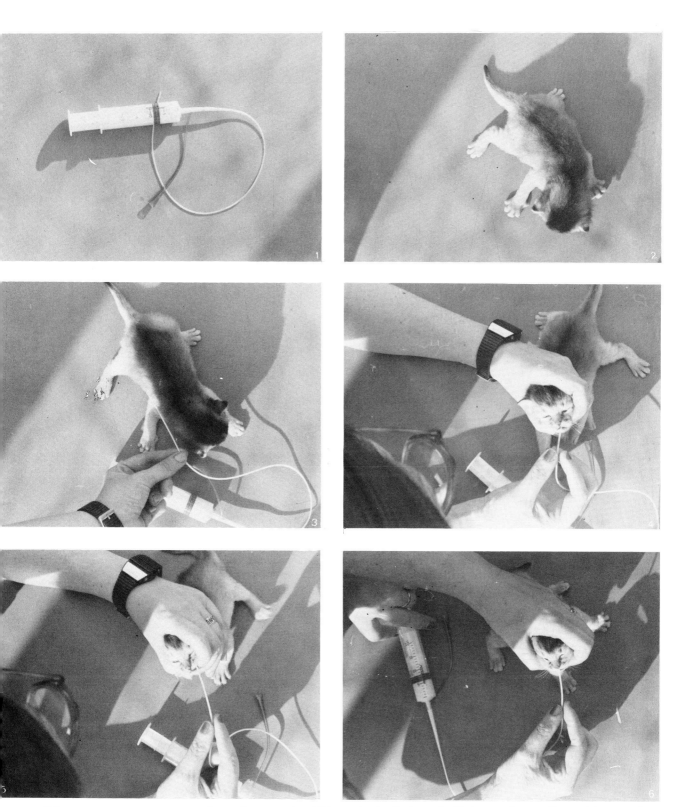

If for some reason a queen refuses to nurse her kittens, try to find a substitute nursing mother cat to complete the task. If this is not possible, the next best thing is to hand feed the kittens using a feeding tube and milk formula. A feeding tube consists of a thin catheter (tube) that has been attached to a syringe (1). (*Note:* There is a second larger tube pictured that can be attached to the syringe instead of the narrower tube. This larger tube is used to hand feed sick or elderly adult cats.) Place the kitten on a table top (2), and using the catheter, measure from the kitten's nose to its last rib to determine how far to insert the feeding tube through the kitten's mouth into its stomach (3). Push all of the air out of the tube first. Then, hold the kitten firmly with one hand and pry open its mouth with your thumb and index finger while inserting the feeding tube with the other hand (4). Insert the tube to the pre-measured length and hold it in place while someone else dispenses the milk from the syringe (5). (*Note:* One person can also manage to feed a kitten without the help of an assistant.)

Left: Gr. Ch. Anshent-won's Mesabi stepping out in style. Breeders/owners: Dr. and Mrs. John W. Boyd (Joyce Chang). **Below:** Avenue Pepi-Kyenne of Nepenthes, a neutered male, pictured at five months. He portrays that wild look so characteristic of Abyssinians. Breeders: Duane and Hertha Chellevold. Owners: Joan and Alfred Wastlhuber. **Opposite:** Wide-eyed and alert is Gr. Ch. El Qahira's Chocolet pictured at six weeks. Breeder/owner: Rae Ann Christ.

The kittens should be fed six times a day for the first two weeks and then four times a day until they are weaned.

Feed about 8 ml. of formula per ounce of body weight a day. A little experience will tell you how much is enough.

The genital region of each kitten must be rubbed, as previously described, to stimulate defecation and urination. Constipation can be treated by adding more Karo syrup to the formula; if diarrhea occurs, the amount of syrup should be reduced. Always protect the kittens from chilling.

By three weeks of age, the kittens should weigh approximately 300 to 350 grams; by seven weeks of age, they should weigh 700 to 800 grams.

COMPOSITION OF QUEEN'S MILK COMPARED TO SUBSTITUTE PRODUCTS

Nutrient	Queen's Milk	KMR	Evap. Milk	Unilact
Water (%)	81.8	82.0	80.0	84.0
Solids (%)	18.2	18.0	20.0	16.0
Protein (%)	9.5	7.5	5.6	5.3
Fat (%)	6.8	4.5	6.4	6.4
Lactase (%)	10.0	4.8	8.1	2.7
Calories (per 100 grams)	142.0	91.4	115.0	90.0
Calcium (mg./100 ml.)	35.0	200.0	271.0	—
Phosphorus (mg./100 ml.)	70.0	165.0	216.0	—

A Successful Home-produced Formula

1 cup evaporated milk
1 cup water
1 tablespoon light Karo syrup
1 egg yolk
1 dropper multiple vitamins

Growing Up

By the time the kittens are four weeks old, they will be able to walk around and explore their environment. Their mother no longer has to initiate nursing, and she will begin to spend some time away from the kittening box. Continue to weigh the kittens daily, if possible, but now that the kittens have some body fat as reserve, a loss or lack of weight gain can be tolerated much better.

At six weeks of age, introduce solid food (commercially prepared foods, as opposed to mother's milk) and the litter box (the queen will stop consuming the waste products of the kittens once they leave an all-milk diet). At first it will seem like the kittens ingest more cat litter than food, but that will change.

The best method of hand feeding orphaned or rejected kittens is with a syringe and catheter arrangement; however, if these items are not readily available, pet nurser kits (complete with bottle and nipples) can be purchased at most pet shops. Bottle feeding is a more time-consuming process, but it may save a kitten's life.

The first foods should consist of meat-vegetable or meat-starch baby foods; do not feed a straight meat product. Begin by smearing a little of the food on the kittens' mouths so that they can taste it. (Abys seem to learn to lap liquids *after* they eat solid food, so I introduce evaporated milk at about seven weeks.)

Gradually encourage the mother to wean the kittens by separating them from her for increasing lengths of time. As the kittens become hungry, they will eat more adult food. By 12 weeks, the transition from dependence on mother to independence should be complete.

The kittens' permanent teeth are cut during the fourth to sixth month, and the deciduous teeth are gradually lost as this occurs. Swelling, tenderness, and redness of the gums may be apparent. Soft foods will help to overcome any loss of appetite which may occur.

During the growth process, Abyssinians should be given a lot of stimulation in the form of toys and attention. This is essential for the development of a good personality, which is one of the most endearing features of the unique Abyssinian.

115

Abys love to be a part of almost everything their owner does, including gift wrapping activities.

Opposite:
Pictured at one year is Ch. Bromide Neptunium.
Breeders/owners: Kate and Karl Faler.

Necklace markings and dark leg barring have been virtually bred out of top show-quality Abyssinians, after years of hard work. Gr. Ch. Anshent-won Gauguin. Breeders/owners: Dr. and Mrs. John W. Boyd (Joyce Chang).

Genetics

by Karl Faler and Kate Faler

Coat Color and the Abyssinian

The color of an Abyssinian's skin and hair is determined by a pigment granule called melanin. It is formed in cells called melanocytes from tyrosine and possibly tryptophan (both amino acids) by the enzyme tyrosinase, which the cells contain in varying levels. The code for the level of tyrosinase is determined by an Abyssinian's color genes.

Biosynthesis of Pigments

Tryptophan has been proposed as the precursor to phaeomelanin due to in-vitro (tissue culture) studies. This seems unlikely, as studies with tryptophan C^{14} show that no radioactive material was incorporated into pigments in-vivo.

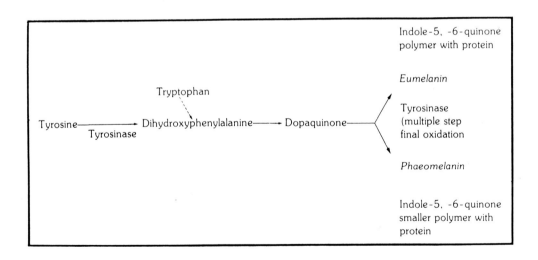

There are two forms of melanin granules. Some appear as brown to black and are called eumelanins; the other type is termed phaeomelanin and looks reddish orange in color. The type and pattern of melanin production is determined genetically. The rusty-red colored parts of ruddy and red Abys indicate that the type of melanin present is phaeomelanin. The granule size, shape, arrangement, and location may be varied to result in a difference in color.

Left: Gr. Ch. Nepenthes Peprika. **Breeders:** Joan and Alfred Wastlhuber. Owners: Tom and Sheila Leaman. **Below:** Ten-month-old Ch. Nepenthes Akime, CFA's Best Aby and Ninth Best Cat, 1980. Breeders/owners: Joan and Alfred Wastlhuber. **Opposite:** Gr. Ch. Spartacus Benediction I, a ruddy male. By Gr. Ch. Queen Tiye's Kaifossus of Ursis x Ch. Scarlett Red Lace of Spartacus. Breeders/owners: Ruth Bauer and Lissa Fried.

Mechanism

If the melanin granules are round, then they have a maximum surface area to absorb light. As no light is being reflected back to the eye, they will appear black (as in the bands of black on the hair of ruddy Abys). If, however, the granules are modified to an oval or football shape (shredded), then they will reflect some light to the eye and appear brown. Hence, the black color has been diluted to brown as seen in red Abys. Red Abyssinians are, thus, not true "red cats" but diluted ruddies. The diluter gene reduces the rate of melanin production, which changes the shape and amount of pigment present. The result, again, is that the black bands appear brown. The rusty-red stripes that alternate with the brown also may be diluted, resulting in a more apricot tone. This same system produces the chocolate point Siamese, as differentiated from the seal point.

Genetically, cats come in two basic colors—red and black. All other colors are modifications of these two. Each one is carried on the "X" chromosome. If a cat has two "X" chromosomes, it will be a female; if it has an "X" chromosome and a "Y" chromosome, it will be a male. Combining red and black results in tortoiseshell cats which are always female because they must combine an "X" carrying red with an "X" carrying black. White cats are the result of a lack of pigment in the skin and hair.

Both ruddy and red ticking cannot appear on the same Abyssinian cat (tortoiseshell) unless the gene has been introduced by crossing with another breed. This indicates that the inheritance pattern is not the same as it is in other red cats, such as Persians. In addition, the incidence of red operates as a simple recessive and is not linked to the sex of the individual.

This is additional evidence that in Abyssinians, the inheritance system or mechanism is dilution of color as seen in the Siamese and not the red of other breeds (see Shaw, 1964 and 1977, for details).

Ruddy and Red Relationships

Many Aby breeders like to produce an occasional red kitten; others wish to concentrate on one color or the other. It is essential that the transmission of the diluter gene is completely understood by those who would like to predict the occurrence of coat color in kittens.

Below are charts depicting possible crosses and their resulting kittens. "R" will represent ruddy genes and "r" will represent red genes. Ruddy is dominant to red. (Note that the sex of the parents has no effect.)

Sire (Ruddy)

Dam (Ruddy)	R	R
R	RR	RR
R	RR	RR

Both parents carry ruddy genes only, (homozygous = RR or rr), and all resulting kittens will be ruddy.

(Incross)

Sire (Red)

Dam (Red)	r	r
r	rr	rr
r	rr	rr

Both parents carry the red gene only and all offspring will be red.

(Incross)

Sire (Ruddy)

Dam (Ruddy)	R	r
R	RR	Rr
r	rR	rr

Both parents carry the red gene, but appear ruddy (heterozygous = Rr). One-quarter of the kittens will be genetically ruddy (RR), one-quarter red (rr), and one-half will be ruddy which carry the red (Rr).★

(Intercross)

★ These figures are based on a statistical analysis of a large population. Individual litters may vary. (For instance, we once had a ruddy queen that was bred to a ruddy sire; both carried the red. The resulting litter was three red kittens and one ruddy. The chances of this occurring are quite small.)

Sire (Ruddy)

Dam (Ruddy)	R	r
R	RR	Rr
R	RR	Rr

Sire carries the red gene, but dam does not. All kittens will be ruddy, but one-half will carry the red.

(Backcross)

Who could resist a face like this? Gr. Ch. Crescent Dantara of Amadear. Breeder: Henrietta Shirk. Owners: Dr. and Mrs. Duane E. Young.

Opposite:
Ch. Bromide Neptunium is proud to pose with his breeders/owners Kate and Karl Faler.

Sire (Ruddy)

Dam (Red)	R	R	Sire is ruddy and dam is red. All kittens appear ruddy but carry the red gene.
r	Rr	Rr	
r	Rr	Rr	(Cross)

Sire (Ruddy)

Dam (Red)	R	r	Sire is ruddy but carries the red and dam is red. One-half of the kittens will carry the red gene but be ruddy and the other half will be red.
r	Rr	rr	
r	Rr	rr	

(Backcross or Testcross)

It is possible to determine the genes of the parents based on the color of the kittens. If two ruddies are mated and red kittens occur, then the parents both must carry the red trait. If only ruddy kittens result, one may carry red and the other not, or both may not. To test if a ruddy Aby carries the red trait, breed it to a red Aby. You can be sure it carries red, if red kittens are produced. If all the resulting kittens are ruddy, then it probably does not carry the red trait. The greater the number of kittens produced, the more certain you can be.

Once the genes of the parents are known, the color of further kittens can be predicted with some accuracy.

Agouti Ticking

Abys are unique among domestic cats in their coloring. The back, head, tail, and outside of the legs are covered with hair that has agouti ticking (each individual hair has from four to six bands of coloring on it). These bands are black in the ruddy Abyssinian or brown in the red Abyssinian, and they alternate with a rusty-red color. This agouti hair pattern is found in many wild animals, where it acts as a natural camouflage. The agouti ticking is determined by a gene called "agouti" which, if not present, will result in solid color.

In Abyssinians, the agouti pattern is seen without the striping that is found in other varieties of ticked cats such as tabbies. The ticking pattern is produced by a gene which has a shredding effect on the melanin granules (the difference between ruddy and red) and by alternately high and low concentrations of the tyrosinase enzyme necessary to produce melanin from tyrosine (causing the banding pattern of the hair itself). Some

126

believe that the Abyssinian was produced through systematic selection of tabby cats that were poorly patterned, resulting in a cat with no stripes but an occasional problem with barring on the legs and the throat area.

Pedigree Analysis

Cats are judged on their physical appearance by breeders and show judges. Genetically speaking, physical appearance is called the *phenotype*, which is composed of two equally important contributors. First, the environment influences a cat's appearance. No cat fancier is likely to argue against the fact that grooming, diet, housing, and so forth can make a difference in the show ring. These factors are usually apparent and can be easily altered to help Abys look their best. The second contributor, however, is the actual genetic makeup of the cat; this is known as the *genotype*, and it is not as readily identified.

The best source for genetic information is a cat's pedigree. This important piece of paper lists a cat's parents, grandparents, greatgrandparents, and so on. It is usually signed by the cat's breeder(s) to make it valid. For the novice, reading a pedigree is no easy task, and the overall effect may be impressive but meaningless; consequently, it is not taken as seriously as it should be, and many cats selected for breeding are evaluated on their phenotype without consideration of genotype.

Names of Cats. A cat's name is made up of several parts. The first word (prefix) is the name of the cattery where the cat was bred. For example, the famous Aby Pharoh Rameses II was bred by Pharoh Cattery. The second word is the cat's "call-name," the name by which it is referred to in the cattery. (It has been our experience that, in addition, many breeders have a variety of pet names or nicknames for their cats, so these are often used when referring to the Aby in place of the "call-name.") The third part (suffix) of the cat's name is added if the cat is sold to another cattery. The suffix consists of the new owner's cattery name and is preceded by the word "of." Aberdeen's Tweed of Blue Iris, thus, was born in Aberdeen Cattery but sold to Blue Iris Cattery. Another cattery name is not added after this, no matter how many owners the Abyssinian has.

When evaluating a pedigree, it is good practice to look for cattery names. By looking through the list of CFA grand champions and All-American winners at the end of this section, you can get an idea of some of the top catteries that are producing outstanding stock.

Breeding Strategies. Another item to evaluate when examining a pedigree is the occurrence of specific cats. Notice if the same cats appear on both the sire's and dam's sides. Determine how many common ancestors your Aby has in each generation.

Outbreeding is the mating of unrelated individuals or those not closely related. This practice has the advantage of introducing new vigor into the lines but it also can produce kittens

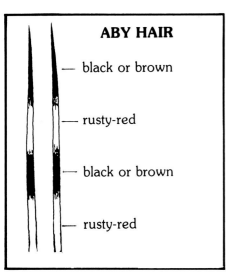

ABY HAIR

— black or brown

— rusty-red

— black or brown

— rusty-red

Two individual hairs that depict the agouti pattern, which gives Abyssinians their characteristic ticked coats.

Left: Cafra Ruth, the progeny of Ch. Avenue Ankh of Cafra and Ch. Hey-Cats Nefer. Breeders: Mr. and Mrs. Lewis Fineman. **Below:** Ch. Dar-Ling Krishtana of Nepenthes, D.M., pictured at two years, is the dam of Gr. Ch. Nepenthes Leo. Breeders: Beverly and Tim Childs. Owners: Joan and Alfred Wastlhuber. **Opposite:** Dbl. Ch. Du-Ro-Al's Gorgeous George of Nephrani, a ruddy Somali and the winner of many awards. See the Somali chapter for more information about this striking longhaired version of the Abyssinian. Breeder: Alma Cowell. Owners: Ruth and Bob Morris.

that are not uniform; in other words, the offspring may be variable in appearance. Many breeders begin with unrelated cats when developing a line, as they can select the occasional outstanding individual and then inbreed to produce their unique cattery "strain."

Inbreeding occurs when related individuals are mated. This practice tends to decrease variation and stabilize phenotype. It is by this method that all pure breeds were originally developed. Intense inbreeding, however, eventually may create health problems, and it leads to the occurrence of undesirable traits (such as some recessive genes) which are more likely to be expressed as they are doubled, tripled, and so on. The amount of inbreeding can be calculated for those interested, but this involves some relatively advanced mathematics (Gardner, 1972).

Many breeders try to balance these strategies (outbreeding and inbreeding) by linebreeding. This involves mating Abyssinians that are related but not closely enough to bring out the problem recessive genes such as tail kinks and toe faults.

Famous Abyssinians. The last thing that can easily be determined when examining a pedigree is the occurrence of Abyssinians of high quality. Note the number of champions (usually abbreviated Ch.) and grand champions (usually abbreviated Gr. Ch.) appearing in the pedigree. These cats have earned their titles by being evaluated by many expert judges who are highly trained for this task. The real purpose of these titles is to make such selected individuals easily recognizable. In addition, look for regional and national award winners.

Selection of a Breeding Population

Good selection of breeding stock begins with establishing a goal. This could be short-term, such as the elimination of leg bars, or long-term, as in meeting the standard of a cat registering association as closely as possible. Whatever you seek, it must be done by objectively eliminating (selling) any Abys that do not measure up to a minimum level. This level must be constantly reviewed and upgraded with the ultimate goal in mind. The process is known as applying "selection pressure." Not following this method will assure reduced rates of improvement and genetic stagnation. Serious breeders seldom can allow emotional attachment to sway any of their judgments when selecting breeding stock.

Selection pressure on males is much greater than on females because a single male may produce (sire) hundreds of kittens in a year, whereas a female seldom has more than ten. It might then be said that such a male should have ten times the selection pressure applied as on the dam.

A good method of applying selection pressure in a cattery involves the culling index. This index consists of a periodic evaluation of each Abyssinian's individual qualities in a numerical chart form. The chart must be constructed by each breeder according to his or her own goals, but the steps are outlined below:

1. List all the Abyssinian qualities you consider important.
2. Weigh the value of each quality, such as Important = 3, Somewhat Important = 2, and Little Importance = 1.
3. Make a scale against which you can evaluate each of these qualities in your cats. For example: Poor = 1, Fair = 2, Good = 3, and so forth.
4. Each quality is given a numerical value by multiplying step 2 by step 3.
5. A minimum cull value is set by the breeder. Those cats that fall below this value are not used for breeding. As your stock improves, this number can then be gradually increased.

An example of a culling index is included for reference and several Abys have been evaluated against it.

CULLING INDEX

Quality (step 1)	Weight* (step 2)	Aby A**	Aby B	Aby C	Aby D
Health	4	4 × 4 = 16	12	16	8
Coat color	3	3 × 2 = 6	6	15	3
Coat texture	2	2 × 3 = 6	6	6	4
Fertility	1	1 × 5 = 5	1	4	2
Head shape	3	3 × 4 = 12	15	12	6
Type	4	4 × 4 = 16	20	16	4
Legs & feet	2	2 × 2 = 4	8	8	6
Tail	1	1 × 3 = 3	4	5	3
Ear (shape, size, & set)	3	3 × 2 = 6	12	12	6
Eyes (color, shape & size)	2	2 × 3 = 6	8	4	8
Clarity	4	4 × 4 = 16	16	12	4
Temperament	1	1 × 4 = 4	1	3	2
Pedigree	3	3 × 4 = 12	15	15	3
Offspring (Quality)	4	4 × 4 = 16	16	20	4
Balance	3	3 × 4 = 12	12	12	6
Totals	—	—	—	—	—
	40	140	152	160	69

(40 × 5 = 200 possible)

*Each quality was weighted according to this scale: 1 = Desirable; 2 = Important; 3 = Very Important; 4 = Essential.

**Abys were evaluated by this index: 1 = Poor; 2 = Fair or Average; 3 = Good; 4 = Very good; 5 = Excellent.

If the cattery in this example set the selection pressure at 100, then Aby D would have to be eliminated from the breeding population. If set at 150, both Abys A and D should be neutered.

Pedigrees that contain a high percentage of grand champion and champion cats reveal those catteries that are producing outstanding show stock. **Opposite above:** Gr. Ch. Scarlett Cain of Puklat. Breeder: Nelly Poole. Owner: Pat Webber. **Opposite below:** Gr. Ch. Anshent-won Gauguin. Breeders/owners: Dr. and Mrs. John W. Boyd (Joyce Chang). **Above:** Dbl. Gr. Ch. Amadear Orianna. Breeders/owners: Dr. and Mrs. Duane E. Young.

CFA Grand Champions and All-American Winners

As a general rule, the more "famous" Abys that occur on a pedigree, the better it is. A list of CFA grand champions and All-American winners follows in order to assist readers in recognizing these Abyssinians. The breeders of these cats have worked hard to produce quality and they know that much time and effort will be saved if a breeder starts with the excellent foundation stock that has been provided.

CFA GRAND CHAMPIONS

1958 - No Abyssinians received Grand Champion status.
1959 - No Abyssinians received Grand Champion status.
1960 - Selene's Vignette of Willouise
1961 - Selene's Tammy of Aberdeen
     Selene's Firefly
     Chirn Sa-Hai Twenty Carats
1962 - Sheramain T. Twinks of Aberdeen
     All-American: Best Aby Female—Ch. Star of Pallady
1963 - Ronnviken's Tutankhamon (Imp.)
1964 - Parkan's Atum
     Willouise Robin of Selene
1965 - Pharoh Rameses II
     Second Highest Scoring Male, All Star Award*, 1966
     All-American: 1967 - Third Best Cat
               1966 - Best Cat
               1965 - Second Best Cat
     Selene's Skylark of Mar-Jon
     Selene's Venita
     Hermcrest Lilo
     Aberdeen's Fire Ball
1966 - Pallady's Sun Song
     Best Aby Female, All Star Award*
     Parkan's Hept
     Best Ruddy Aby Female, All Star Award*
     Selene's Menes of Nile
     Sheramain Yankee Sultan of Du-Ro-Al
     Other Winners (CFA): Best Red Aby Male—Ch. Fredna's Flame-Beau of Kai
1967 - Aberdeen's Tweed of Blue Iris
     Willouise Royal Gold of Sherdon
     Abi Abdol of Selene
     Aida's Miss Merry Kissmas
     Chota-Li R.S.T.

*Hydon-Goodwin
 All Star Award
**Short-haired

A show judge examines the profile of this entry.

A second place rosette adorns the cage of entry 56.

Mar-Jon's Ariel
    Best Aby Female (CFA)
Pallady's Fyrfli
Pallady's Bravo
Seit of D'Nel
Willouise Royal Gold of Sherdon
Other Winners (CFA): Best Red Aby—Will's Gold
    Digger

1968 - Amulet's Amenhotep of Van-Lyn
        Best Aby Opposite Sex (CFA)
        Second Best Aby, All Star Award*
    Selene's Muezza of Amulet
    Amulet's Scheherazade
    Chota-Li Russet
        Best Aby (CFA)
        Second Best S.H.** Female, All Star Award*
    Crestline's Thunderball
    Kobold of Blue-Iris (Imp.)
    Du-Ro-Al Sorrel Sioux
        Best Red Aby (CFA)
    Selene's Meresa of Nile
    Wah-Lee Abigail of Yang-Le
    Wohl-Rabe's Tira of Hasmid
    All Star Award Winners:
        Best Red Female—Ch. Du-Ro-Al Sorrel Sioux
        of Pallady
        Best Red Male—Ch. Wohl-Rabe's Rufa

1969 - Temas Pride of Pharoh (Junior)
        Fifth Best Cat, All Star Award*
    Chota-Li Flair
        Second Best S.H.** Female, All Star Award*
    Amulet's Princess Tana
    Cairo's Kizan of Amulet
        Best S.H.** Male, All Star Award*
        Best Aby (CFA)
    Cher-Lan's Bilichi
    All Star Award Winner:
        Best Red Aby—Juvenile Red Baroness

1970 - Chota-Li Fiesta of Fongin
    Selene's Robin
    Temas Ramesa
    Temas Hot Shot of Pallady
    Amulet's Pepi of Nepenthes
        Second Best Cat All Breed, All Star Award*
        Best Kitten All Breed

*Hydon-Goodwin
All Star Award
**Short-haired

135

Gr. Ch. El Qahira's Darius II. Breeder/ owner: Rae Ann Christ. Only cats that have completed requirements for grand championship are awarded this title as a name prefix.

Cairo's Katie of Holiday Hill
Mirkwood Crispin
Quin Jo's Katari of Ra Da Lu
    Best Aby Female, All Star Award*
Avenue Tuk-Rainier of Etta-Mert
Cairo's Tut of Nefer-Abby
Mar-Jon's Firefly
Mel-End's Little Bradley of Aida
Singing River Thunderbird
Van Dyke's Abi Tina of D'Nel
Other Winners (CFA):
    Best Red Aby Male—Ch. David Copperfield of
    LeRoux
1971 - Amulet's Ankha of Ja-Bob
Pusca's El Bardari
Holiday Hill Man O'War of Pharoh
Chota-Li Kahina of Phalkon
Jeannel Charlie
    Best Aby (CFA)
Rubaiyat Sheenah
Aida's 'Twas
Whol-Rabe's Hadji-Baba of Ma-Jah
Mirkwood Gaston of Abyiat
Van Dyke Abi Somali of Pyramid
Crestline's Thunder Chile
Crestline's Toughie Mouse
Hai-Tael's Firebrand
Wohl-Rabe's Zakari of Hi-Ab
Wohl-Rabe's Abdel Simbal of Andor
Amulet's Adonis
Chota-Li Sienna of Quin-Jo
1972 - Gallantree's Casey Jones
    Third Best Cat, Midwest Region, 1973
Gallantree's Davey Jones
Pharoh Citation of Swingate
    Best Cat, All Breed, 1973
    Best Aby, 1973
Chota-Li Mia
Chota-Li Cricket of Phaulkon
    Eighth Best Cat, Southwest Region, 1973
Three Crown Taco
Ma-Jah Ugas
Jeannel B.C. of Maou
Ro-B-L Don Juan of Peck's
Invictus of Blue Iris

Gr. Ch. Jeannel Charlie. Breeder/owner: Donna Jean Thompson.

*Hydon-Goodwin
All Star Award
**Short-haired

138

Gr. Ch. Jo Bo's Pojoaque of Los Colorados, a red male. Breeder: Mrs. D. O. Bomar. Owner: Marilyn Fuentes Sumner.

Gr. Ch. El Qahira's Deseret. Breeder/owner: Rae Ann Christ.

Rusty Red of Eriador
    Best Red Aby, 1973
Walmar's Luna of Queen Tiye
D'As-Shing's Shane of Aberdeen
Eriador's Sheikh of Amulet
Etta-Mert Farmer Girl
Etta-Mert Rhonda
Etta-Mert Trumpeter
David Copperfield of LeRoux
Mirkwood Gaston of Abyiat
    Best Aby
    Fourth Best Cat
Pallady Gabrielle
Walmar's Luna of Queen Tiye
Pharoh Ginger of Bobbi-Jean
Malkata Rhubarb
Wohl-Rabe's Irish of Robson
1973 – El Qahira's Deseret
    Fourth Best Cat, Midwest Region, 1974
Eriador's Pippin II
Genandra's Alex
Gallantree's Hot Pants
Gaine's Penelope of Pussy-Pur-Mew
Jo Bo's Pojoaque of Los Colorados
Purrong's Bir-Han
Quin-Jo's Cassandra
Wohl-Rabe's Warlock of Scarlett

*Hydon-Goodwin
All Star Award
**Short-haired

139

Ch. Nepenthes Akime, pictured at eight weeks (**left**) and Gr. Ch. Nepenthes Leo (**below**). Breeders/owners: Joan and Alfred Wastlhuber. **Opposite:** Gr. Ch. Anshent-won That Cat. Breeders/owners: Dr. and Mrs. John W. Boyd (Joyce Chang).

1974 – Abu Simbel Tars Tarkas of Helium
    Abyiat's Saskia of Gallantree
    Amulet's Malaika of Anshent-Won
        Eighth Best Cat, Northwest Region
    Avenue Alexander of Lyn-Li
    Crescent Dantara of Amadear
    El Qahira's Chocolet
    Gallantree's Hobie Cat
        Fourth Best Kitten, Midwest Region, 1973
    Gallantree's Kristy
    Gallantree's Lancer
    Koshan's M. Paco
    Pallady's Native Dancer
        Sixth Best Cat, Gulf Shore Region
    Queen Tiye's Renaissance of Owen
        Sixteenth Best Cat, All Breed
        Third Best Cat, Gulf Shore Region
        Best Kitten, Gulf Shore Region
        Best Aby
        Seventh Best Cat, Gulf Shore Region, 1975
    Quin-Jo's Brass Tacks
    Rallim's Cayenne
    Etta-Mert Pilot
    Kilborn's Pink Chablis
        Best Red Aby

*Hydon-Goodwin
  All Star Award
**Short-haired

Gr. Ch. Queen Tiye's Renaissance of O-Wen, CFA's Best Abyssinian and 16th Best Cat, 1974. By Gr. Ch. Chota-Li R.S.T. x Gr. Ch. Walmar's Luna of Queen Tiye. Breeder: Jean Soper. Owners: Kerry and Carolyn Owen.

Gr. Ch. El Qahira's Chocolet. Breeder/owner: Rae Ann Christ.

Gr. Ch. Bastis Zackariah, D.M. Breeders/owners: Wain Harding and Bob Chorneau.

1975 - Anshent-Won's Anasazi
Anshent-Won's Makeba
Bastis Zackariah
Third Best Cat, Southern Region, 1976
Cafra Honeysuckle
Cafra Aurora
Colbyshire Cochise of Quin-Jo
Best Aby
Seventh Best Cat, Great Lakes Region
Companion Cat Neb En Sebau
Best Red Aby
Etta-Mert Town Talk of Phaulkon
Fifth Best Cat, Southwest Region
Gallantree's Out Rider
Genandra's Cin-Ful Cinnamon
Golden Ra's Temu
Golden Ra's Keb
Koshan Nak'
Mai-Tel-A Hot Spur
Queen Tiye's Jessica
Quin Jo's Freya
Quin Jo's Shendi of J-Lore
Eighth Best Cat, Great Lakes Region
Eighth Best Cat, Great Lakes Region, 1976
Sundance Abou Krishna
Mau Jokers Wild
1976 - Anshent-Won's Maya of Gallantree
Amadear Orianna
Avenue Pepi-Tbasko of Nepenthes
Tenth Best Cat
Second Best Cat, Northwest Region
Bastis Face to Face
Bastis Glitters N' Glows
Cyan's R.P.L.
Cyan's Kodachrome of Helium
El Qahira's Hot Toddy
Ninth Best Cat, Midwest Region
Best Ruddy Aby, 1977
Seventh Best Cat, Midwest Region, 1977
El Qahira's Sharm El
Best Aby
Seventh Best Cat
Second Best Cat, Midwest Region
Etta-Mert Mitchell
Etta-Mert Foreglow
Etta-Mert Tamarack
Etta-Mert Trademark of Orca

*Hydon-Goodwin
All Star Award
**Short-haired

143

Etta-Mert Trader
Faraway's Buffo Sibu
Los Colorado's Amiga
    Best Aby, 1977
    Best Red Aby, 1977
    Fourth Best Cat, Gulf Shore Region, 1977
Mara-Ty Teak
Queen Tiye's Demet of Koshan
Quin-Jo's Sienna
Queen Tiye's Kaifossus of Ursis
Scarlett Dan D. Lion of Bastis
Scarlett Pimpernel of Sangpur
Sun Dance Monisa of Eairywind
Sun Dance Sarva
Thieroff's Flash Farkel
    Best Red Aby
    Seventh Best Cat, Gulf Shore Region
Three Crown Tafari
Three Crown Sunny Jim
Abu Simel's Lady

Gr. Ch. Quin-Jo's Cardinal, CFA's Ninth Best Cat, 1979. By Gr. Ch. Bastis Zackariah, D.M. x Ch. Quin-Jo's Paprika, D.M. Breeders/owners: Rich and Becky Jones.

*Hydon-Goodwin
 All Star Award
**Short-haired

Gr. Ch. El Qahira's Hot Toddy. Breeder/
owner: Rae Ann Christ.

1977 - Abi-Kaftan of Rendale
Abizaq Penda
Abu Simbel's Oliver Twist of Syba
Anshent-Won Anahita
Anshent-Won Margaux
Anshent-Won's Manani of Soketumi
   Third Best Cat, North Atlantic Region, 1978
   Second Best S.H.** Cat, 1978
   Eleventh Best Cat, 1978
Anshent-Won's Mesabi
Badfinger's Lyon of Darken
Catalpa's Saffron
Chula Ban Wild Fire of Sun Dance
Colbyshire's Chippewa of Essyx
Faraway Akaikane Chollima
Golden Ra's Kachina of Shady Paws
Jest-O Mister O
Jest-O Tobias
Mara-Ty Love Child of Nectarine
Morningside Buzz
Nepenthes Leo
   Tenth Best Cat, Northwest Region
   Best Kitten, Northwest Region
   Sixth Best Cat, Northwest Region, 1978
Nepenthes Tquilla of Badfinger
O-Wen's Latigo
O-Wen's Macho
Quin-Jo's Butternut of Sunnerise
Red Jefferson of Yala
Rubaiyat Wakabu of Hutzler
Ruddy Raider of Wil-O-Glen
Queen Tiye's Gold
Saika Shams Sabrina Fair
Scarlett Cain of Puklat
Scarlett Heathcliff
Scarlett Steppenwolf
Bastis Panama Red
   Seventh Best Cat, Southern Region
   Fifth Best Cat, Southern Region, 1978
   Nineteenth Best Cat, 1978
Etta-Mert Brigadier
Etta-Mert Brigadoon
Anshent-Won's Ariba of Soketumi
1978 - Adhajon's Bam-Bam Calli Bama
Anshent-Won Gauguin
Anshent-Won That Cat
Avenue Koko Amenhotep of Jocar

*Hydon-Goodwin
All Star Award
**Short-haired

Badfinger's Bumble Bee
    Eigth Best Cat, Southern Region
Badfinger's Genesis of Catknapp
    Eighth Best Cat, Southwest Region, 1981
Cyan's Kodacolor of Helium
El Qahira's Darius II
El Qahira's Jubilee of Lapinchat
Fellow's Copper Flash of Mara-Ty
Helium's Misfire
Hocuspocus Harry Houdini
J-Lore's Carrisa
J-Lore's Kim Ombo
Lakme Kahalil Gibran
Magdelen of Fellows
Nepenthes DuBonnet
Nepenthes Khari of Shagrat
Nepenthes Peprika
Nepenthes Prophet of Dar-Ling
Orca's Tatoosh
Pashaka's Lord Yabu
Phaulkon's Ezzedin
    Fifth Best Cat, Southwest Region
Quin-Jo's Pietro
    Third Best Cat, Great Lakes Region
Romira Kipling of Shagrat
Soketumi Samadari
    Third Best Cat, 1979
    Second Best Kitten, North Atlantic Region
Sun Dance Cheyenne Autumn
Sunnerise Laburnum of Erinwood
Sunnerise Beechnut
    Fifth Best Cat, Great Lakes Region
Telika
Ursis Nunzio
Valley's Chandler
Willard's Ras Tafari Ras Rases
Nile's the Wild One V of Glasgow
1979 – Abizaq Rustique
Anshent-Won's Dagda
Badfinger's Bumin' Around TQ
Badfinger's Kalua of Avelion
Badfinger's Kandy Kiss of Gemtone
Biwako
El Qahira's Shasu II
    Fourth Best Cat, Midwest Region, 1980
El Qahira's Snezek

Gr. Ch. El Qahira's Zagnut, sired by Gr. Ch. Bastis Zackariah, D.M. Breeder/owner: Rae Ann Christ.

*Hydon-Goodwin
All Star Award
**Short-haired

Gr. Ch. Nepenthes Narcissa II of Spartacus, a ruddy female. By Gr. Ch. Nepenthes Dubonnet x Ch. Nepenthes Regina. Breeders: Joan and Alfred Wastlhuber. Owners: Ruth Bauer and Lissa Fried.

Gr. Ch. Phaulkon's Kassibi. Breeders/owners: Jim and Sylvia Fitzgerald.

El Qahira's Zagnut
Fellow's Loverly of Jocar
Helium's Supertramp
Kats II Teton of Phancy
Leoca Astra
Los Colorados Padric of Kilaran
Nepenthes Narcissa II
Nepenthes Nereus
    Fourth Best Cat
Phaulkon's Kassibi
Quin-Jo's Cardinal
Rambo's Rapscallion
Rimpoche's Sunshine
Rubaiyat Bengali
Rubaiyat Sanhedrin of Cinemor
Scarlett Chocoletta
Selkhet's Scirrocco
Spartacus Benediction I
Tausert's Kundalini
Triad's Hollywood Hot of Bastis
Wil-O-Glen's Ahmose

Third Best Cat - Gr. Ch. Soketumi Samadari (Second Best Cat, North Atlantic Region)
Fourth Best Cat - Gr. Ch. Nepenthes Nereus (Second Best Cat, Northwest Region)
Ninth Best Cat - Gr. Ch. Quin-Jo's Cardinal (Second Best Cat, Great Lakes Region)

Regional

Sunnerise Laburnum of Erinwood, Seventh Best Cat and Best Red Aby, Northwest Region
Fellow's Loverly of Jocar, Second Best Cat and Best Red Aby, Southwest Region
Phaulkon's Kassibi, Seventh Best Cat, Southwest Region
El Qahira's Darius II, Sixth Best Cat, Midwest Region
Badfinger's Genesis, Best Aby, Southern Region

1980 - Abai Spiderperson
        Abizaq Musique
        Abydos' Phaedra I
        Adhajon's Rubrica
        Amara Nikon
        Eairywind Dahabi Shahin
        El Qahira's Seth
        Fellow's Apollo of Jocar
        Hapidaz' Alexander G.

*Hydon-Goodwin
All Star Award
**Short-haired

Helium's Egeliac Unicket
Lakme Kalahari of Raelich
Nepenthes Akime
Nepenthes Esprit
Phaulkon's Killer Bee
Red Rover
Rubaiyat Panthea
Selkhet's Afternoon Delight
Selkhet's Oraby of Dusdee
Spartacus Bess II
Tausert's Ghunga-Dhin
Vigil's Ghunga Din
Vigil's Ibn Ebn
Abizaq Great Balls O' Fire
Badfinger's Baby Face
Bromide Kye-En of Sirkarah

1980 – Regional Winners
    Abizaq Great Balls O' Fire
        Best Aby, North Atlantic Region
    Nepenthes Akime
        Second Best Cat, Northwest Region
    Nepenthes Esprit
        Best Kitten, Northwest Region
    Abanth's Moondust
        Best Aby, Gulf Shore Region
    Abizaq Musique of Essyx
        Best Aby, Great Lakes Region
    Vigil's Ibn Ebn
        Sixth Best Cat, Southwest Region
    El Qahira's Shasu II
        Fourth Best Cat, Midwest Region
    Badfinger's Bumin' Around TQ
        Seventh Best Cat, Southern Region

1981 – Abizaq Flicka of Badfinger
    Abizaq Red Chequer
    Abydos California Zephyr
    Abydos Phoenix
    Badfinger's Ben Purr of Bojangles
    Badfinger's Zebulon of Starseyn
    Cinna's Jack Daniels
    Cucho's Little Red of Kenipurr
    Holliday's Miam Merit
    Jocar's Pegasus
    Kikidi's Rampar
    Nepenthes Muizzah

*Hydon-Goodwin
 All Star Award
**Short-haired

Nepenthes Pele
Phaulkon's Music Trance
Pooka's Crystal Pallas
Puklat's Rose Fever of Dantre
Soketumi Red Fern of Orch Idee
Tangerine Tijuana Taxi
Tausert's Farenheit 500
Wil-O-Glen's Tyrone
Bastis Bold and Brassy
Eairywind Dahabi Kalila
El Qahira's Dason
Faraway's Phara
Oldetyme's Road Runner
Quin-Jo's Gatico
Sun Dance Indian Summer of Abadulah
Nepenthes Copper of Bromide
Hapidaz's Buck Rogers

Regional
Lakme Kalahari of Raelich, Fourth Best Cat and Best Red
Aby, Northwest Region
Abydos Phoenix, Seventh Best Cat and Best Red Aby,
North Atlantic Region
Badfinger's Zebulon of Starseyn, Sixth Best Cat, Midwest
Region
Cinna's Jack Daniels, Best Cat, and Best Aby,
Midwest Region
Badfinger's Genesis of Catknapp, Eighth Best Cat and
Best Aby, Southwest Region

ALL-AMERICAN WINNERS
(Includes all major associations, except CFA, after 1976)
1966 - Cat of the Year—Pharoh Rameses II
1973 - Cat of the Year—Joelwyn The Wild One III of Nile
1976 - Best Aby—El Qahira's Sharm El
Second Best Aby—Avenue Pepi-Tbasko of Nepenthes
Third Best Aby—Bastis Zackariah
1977 - Best Aby—Nile's Scarlett O'Hara II of Mar-Rob
Second Best Aby—Van Dyke's Abi Abdel
Third Best Aby—Ying Yang's Golden Maya of
Denjobo
Best Red Aby and Fourth Best Aby—Badfinger's
Lyon of Darken
Second Best Red Aby and Fifth Best Aby—
Companion Cat A.D. II of Overland

*Hydon-Goodwin
All Star Award
**Short-haired

Gr. Ch. Anshent-won's Anasazi.
Breeders: Dr. and Mrs. John W. Boyd
(Joyce Chang). Owner: Bob Kreft.

Third Best Red Aby and Sixth Best Aby—
   Jest-O Mister O
1978 - Best Aby—Van Dyke's Abi Abdel
   Second Best Aby—Kats II ReRun of Nile
   Third Best Aby—Mar-Rob's Beau Sonne
   Best Red Aby and Fourth Best Aby—
      Mi-Si-Am Bit-O-Honey of Red Barn
   Second Best Red Aby and Fifth Best Cat—
      Darken's the Red Machine
   Third Best Aby and Sixth Best Cat—Lawndale's
      Lady
1979 - Best Aby—Kats II Teton of Phancy
   Second Best Aby—Wil-O-Glen's Sultan of Sea
      Breeze
   Third Best Aby—Van Dyke's Abi Abou
   Best Red Aby and Fourth Best Aby—
      Ayudhya Red Menelik of Nubian

*Hydon-Goodwin
 All Star Award
**Short-haired

Gr. Ch. Avenue Pepi-Tbasko of Nepenthes, CFA's Tenth Best Cat, 1976. Sire of Gr. Ch. Nepenthes Leo. Breeders: Duane and Hertha Chellevold. Owners: Joan and Alfred Wastlhuber.

Second Best Red Aby and Fifth Best Aby—
   Thieroff's Dyan
Third Best Red Aby and Sixth Best Cat—
   Puklat's Neon Rush of Phancy
1980 - Best Aby—Van Dyke's Abi Abou
   Second Best Aby and Best Red Aby—Ayudhya
      Red Menelik of Nubian
   Third Best Aby—Ballycotton's Misty Harbor
   Fourth Best Aby—Ying Yang Tjasa
   Fifth Best Aby and Second Best Red Aby—
      Flyaway Wildfire
1981 - Best Aby—Ying Yang's Shazam
   Second Best Aby—Dehn's Bojangles
   Third Best Aby and Best Red Aby—
      Soketumi Red Fern of Orch Idee
   Fourth Best Aby—Ballycotton's Misty Harbor
   Fifth Best Aby and Second Best Red Aby—
      Kadi's Remy Martin

*Hydon-Goodwin
All Star Award
**Short-haired

151

The Red Abyssinian

by Jeannette Walder

Red Abyssinians are like good red wine. A person is either a born connoisseur, acquires a "taste" for red Abys, or hates them. I fell in love with red Abys when I saw my first picture of one, Int. Ch. Dockaheems Caresse, in the book *Champion Cats of the World.* From that very day I decided I was going to own, breed, and perpetuate those exquisite red creatures. In contrast, Marge Orsini (Ursis Cattery) went through ten years of breeding ruddies exclusively before she wanted and acquired her first red Aby. Now, of course, she is hooked on them.

Description

The red Abyssinian is identical in every respect to the ruddy except for color. Where the ruddy Aby has black bands of ticking and black or dark brown paw pads, the red has chocolate-brown ticking and rosy pink paw pads. Red kittens are easily identified at birth due to the complete absence of black anywhere on their bodies and the pink paw pads. The ground color on the red is a rich copper-red, with deeper shades preferred in show specimens. However, good ticking is never to be sacrificed for depth of color. Also, there should be a definite color variation between the ticked body color and the unticked lighter belly color. Poor or light ticking has been a problem with the reds and is a show fault. The poorer-ticked reds often appear to be solid red cats and are less striking than well-ticked cats. The reason many people believe ruddies are more striking in appearance than reds is, undoubtedly, because they have not seen a properly ticked red. Good ticking on a red is even more important than on a ruddy.

It has been my experience that although little can be told about a kitten's "type" at birth, much can be told of the kitten's color and ticking. Just as the ruddies that are black all over with bright ruddy faces have the best ticking and color, so do the red kittens that are deep chocolate all over with bright red faces. In other words, the blacker ruddy kittens and the browner red kittens tend to have the best ticking and color. Conversely, a ruddy kitten with black and a red kitten with chocolate-brown only on the tops of their heads and tips of their tails will have poor

Gr. Ch. Los Colorado's Amiga, a female, was the first red Abyssinian to win CFA's Best Aby award, 1977. Breeder/owner: Marilyn Fuentes Sumner.

153

ticking no matter how intense the ruddy or red body color. Dark facial markings tend to go with dark ticking and, of course, are preferred in show specimens.

Genetics

Red Abys are a dilution of the ruddy; genetically, this is known as a simple recessive. What this means is that when two reds are bred together, only red kittens will result. When two homozygous ruddies are bred together, only ruddies will result. When two heterozygous ruddies (ruddies carrying the red gene) are bred together, on the average, 25% of the kittens will be red. When a red is bred to a heterozygous ruddy, on the average, 50% of the kittens will be red.

It is impossible to tell from appearances if a ruddy carries the red gene. It is sometimes also impossible to tell from a pedigree. A ruddy can have nothing but ruddy ancestors for more than *eight* generations and still carry the red gene, or a ruddy can have one red grandparent and *not* carry the red gene. The only way a breeder can be sure a ruddy carries the red gene is (1) if one parent is a red, or (2) if the ruddy has produced a red kitten (See the Genetics chapter).

History

According to renowned Aby breeder and CFA judge Edna Field, the first early red Abys can be traced to three British studs (all ruddy), Bruene Achilles, Nigella Contenti, and Croham Abeba. Most American red Abys can be traced to the British catteries Woodroofe, Croham and Kreeoro. In June, 1952, the Abyssinian Cat Club of America reported the first American-bred red Aby kitten out of Croham Abeba and Taishun Dawn (both ruddies). In 1955, Rufus the Red of Selene was the first red Aby imported to the United States. In 1959, Coleswood Christopher and Raby Honey, the first red-to-red breeding in the United States, produced two red kittens.

Dorothy Winsor was responsible for the recognition of red Abys in England. Marge Pallady and Alma Cowell are largely responsible for their recognition in the United States. Red Abys were officially recognized by the Governing Council of the Cat Fancy (GCCF) in England in 1963 and by the Cat Fanciers' Association (CFA) in the United States in 1964.

In 1966, Pallady's Sun Song, a red female bred and owned by Marge Pallady, became the first CFA grand champion red Aby. In 1977, Los Colorado's Amiga, a red female bred and owned by Marilyn Fuentes, was the first red Aby to win CFA's Best Aby award. In 1978, Bastis Panama Red, a red male bred and owned by Wain Harding, was CFA's Nineteenth Best Cat and the first red Aby to make a Top Twenty win. Also in 1978, Helium's Red Raven of Amara, a red neuter bred by Jeannette Walder and owned by Lorna Malinen, became the first grand premier red Aby. A list of red Aby grands to date appears at the end of this chapter.

Breeding

I saw my first red Aby in 1973. She had a round head, light color, barring and white that extended well below her double necklaces. Many, if not most, of the early reds had similar problems. Since I was a novice breeder and did not know any better, I bought the cat. As it turned out, she could not breed, so she was spayed and placed as a pet. It was not until 1974 that, quite unexpectedly, I got my first good red Aby. I agreed to breed my ruddy stud, Grand Champion Abu Simbel Tars Tarkas of Helium, to Dr. Charles Elfont's ruddy female, Champion Wen'Jen's Naomi of Cyan. Naomi had five kittens, three of which were red. No one was happier than I to learn that Naomi carried red and had given me Grand Champion Cyan's Kodachrome of Helium (I had learned earlier that Tarkas also carried red).

Although Kodachrome bred to my red male, Champion Helium's Ironwolf (a double Tarkas grandson), and produced three red grands (Grand Champion Helium's Misfire, Grand Premier Helium's Red Raven of Amara, and Grand Premier Helium's Spitfire), I quickly realized that the best red generally came from ruddy-to-ruddy or ruddy-to-red breedings. Other red breeders have discovered this also. Two excellent examples of reds out of ruddies are Grand Champion Los Colorado's Amiga, ruddy to red, and Grand Champion Bastis Panama Red, ruddy to ruddy. Both Amiga and Panama, as mentioned earlier, went on to achieve CFA national awards.

Two modern ruddy studs deserve recognition for having produced more red Aby grands than any other red Aby studs (although statistics have a way of making liars out of authors after the book goes to press). Grand Champion Abu Simbel Tars Tarkas of Helium produced Grand Champion Cyan's Kodacolor of Helium and Grand Champion Abizaq Penda. Grand Champion Bastis Zackariah produced Grand Champion Bastis Panama Red, Grand Champion Badfinger's Genesis, and Grand Premier Badfinger's Jasyn of Aswan.

Red Abys were not accepted for a long time by the various cat registering associations, as it is common for cats bred in new colors not to have the following that those with existing colors enjoy; consequently, the gene pool for red is not as large and available specimens generally are not as good. This, coupled with the minimizing effect of red being a recessive gene, makes it very difficult for the reds ever to compete, in any great number, with the ruddies.

Many red breeders have been "breeding" to the ruddies to improve the quality of the reds, and with good results. There is nothing more exciting to a red breeder than to learn that a top-winning ruddy carries red. The reds today are far better specimens than the first red I saw in 1973, and they will continue to get better as the gene pool is expanded both in quantity and quality through breeding with ruddies.

The Future

Are red Abys growing in popularity? Yes, it appears so. As the quality of the reds improves and the exposure to the public increases, they will become more popular.

Will red Abys ever surpass ruddy Abys? Probably not. Will good red wine ever replace Coca-Cola® as our national beverage? Probably not. But good red Abys, like good red wine, will always have a place in our culture.

CFA GRAND CHAMPION RED ABYSSINIANS
(1966 - 1981)

1966
Pallady's Sun Song

1968
Du-Ro-Al Sorrel Sioux of Pallady

1972
D'As-Shing's Shane of Aberdeen
Rusty Red of Eriador
David Copperfield of LeRoux

1973
Gaine's Penelope of Pussy-Pur-Mew
Jo Bo's Pojoaque of Los Colorados

1974
Kilborn's Pink Chablis

1975
Companion Cat Neb En Sebau

1976
Cyan's Kodachrome of Helium
Los Colorado's Amiga
Mara-Ty Teak
Thieroff's Flash Farkel

1977
Abizaq Penda
Badfinger's Lyon of Darken
Chula Ban Wild Fire of Sun Dance
Faraway Akaikane Chollima
Jest-O Mister O
Red Jefferson of Yala
Bastis Panama Red

1978
Badfinger's Genesis
Cyan's Kodacolor of Helium
Fellow's Copper Flash of Mara-Ty
Lakme Khalil Gibran
Helium's Misfire
Pashaka's Lord Yabu
Telika

156

Above: Gr. Ch. Thieroff's Flash Farkel, a red male. Breeder/owner: Elaine Thieroff. **Below:** Gr. Ch. Companion Cat Neb En Sebau, a red male, was CFA's Best Red Aby, 1975. Breeder/owner: Pam Black.

1979
Abizaq Rustique
Badfinger's Kandy Kiss of Gemtone
Biwako
Fellow's Loverly of Jocar
Leoca Astra
Los Colorado's Padric of Kilaran
Rimpoche's Sunshine
Triad's Hollywood Hot of Bastis
Rambo's Rapscallion

1980
Abai Spiderperson
Abydos' Phaedra I
Amara Nikon
Fellow's Apollo of Jocar
Lakme Kalahari of Raelich
Red Rover
Abizaq Great Balls O'Fire
Bromide Kye-En of Sirkarah

Gr. Ch. El Qahira's Zagnut. Breeder/owner: Rae
Ann Christ.

1981
Abizaq Flicka of Badfinger
Abizaq Red Chequer
Abydos' California Zephyr
Abydos' Phoenix
Cucho's Little Red of Kenipurr
Jocar's Pegasus
Puklat's Rose Fever of Dantre
Soketumi Red Fern of Orch Idee
Faraway's Phara

CFA GRAND PREMIER RED ABYSSINIANS
(1966 - 1981)

1978
Helium's Red Raven of Amara
1979
Badfinger's Jasyn of Aswan
Helium's Spitfire
Mara-Ty Maple Suger
1980
Amara Red Rollei of Will-Ane
Bastis Fig Newton of Dusdee
1981
Triad's Rusty Nail of Furr-Lo
Rimpoches's Daybreak

Gr. Ch. Foxtail's Big Sky, a Somali. Breeder: Patricia Nell Warren.
Owner: Kate Reinert, Oslo, Norway. Except for its long coat and full,
brush tail, the Somali is very similar in type to the Abyssinian. Both
breeds have uniformly ticked coats and tabby facial markings; both
are medium-sized cats (although the Somali tends to be somewhat
larger) with long, lithe, muscular bodies; and both have heads that
are modified, slightly rounded wedges, topped by large, alert ears.

160

The Somali: A Credit to the Abyssinian Breed

by Patricia Nell Warren

No other new longhair breed has swept to popularity in such a short time as has the Somali. After five years of intensive ground work in CFA, the breed entered CFA championship competition on May 1, 1979. The very first weekend of the season saw Somalis entered as opens in the all-breed finals. At Lancaster, for instance, Lynn-Lee's Desert Fox and Sant'gria's Bolero made finals under Miriam Faulkner and Walter Friend. Fox had been 1978-79 Top Provisional Somali. The very next weekend at Jersey City came the first Best Cat. This was my ruddy male open, Foxtail's Rio Grande. The win was in longhair specialty under Donna Davis. As the summer moved on, two Somalis were running in front for the somewhat ephemeral honor of being the first CFA grand champion.

One of the front runners was Nephrani's Kubla Khan, a red male owned by Ruth and Bob Morris. Khan already had a season behind him, had been Third Best Provisional Somali, and still looked very good. The other was my Rio, who had been Best Provisional Somali kitten. He had just turned eight months and was in his first bloom.

In our eagerness to test the judges' reception of the Somali, the Morrises and I traveled a lot. Our two boys popped up everywhere: Atlanta, Chicago, Rhode Island, and Kansas City. At Toledo and Lexington, both boys made finals together! On August 25, at Cats Plain and Fancy in Boston, Rio topped 200 points to grand. Then, on September 1, at Mountain Empire in Tennessee, Khan granded too.

As grand champions, the two boys kept up their winning streaks. At Westchester, Rio was Best Cat AB, as well as Second Best Cat and Fourth Best Cat. The same weekend, in Elgin, Khan was Best Cat in two specialty rings. By November, Rio had done so well that people encouraged me to run him for the CFA National Awards. Rio came in Nineteenth Best CFA Cat and Sixth Best Cat in the North Atlantic Region. Khan finished in the Midwest Region with a CFA award.

The very special excitement of that first season in CFA championship competition is a memory that all of us will treasure. The Somali, long the stepchild of the Abyssinian, finally had its glass slippers and was on its way to the ball.

As many people know, the Somali is—very simply—a long-haired Abyssinian. The discussions about how and why the longhair gene got into the Aby gene pool have become pretty much academic.

At one time, many Aby breeders said, "Somalis—yuck. Dirty elbows, lots of white, dark roots galore." There was no denying, then, that the Somali had more of the typical Aby problems, but the best Somalis today have clarity, little white, glowing color, and rich ticking.

Part of the Somali's popularity is due to tireless work by pioneer breeders like Evelyn Mague. Like the Oriental Short-hair, the Somali has become a textbook example of how to launch a breed. The work done to promote the breed ranged from pamphlets handed out at cat shows to articles in major cat magazines, to organizing big classes, and to making sure that judges knew the breed. Part of the success is surely due to the growing popularity of the Abyssinian, but, in large amounts, the Somali's success is due to the cat itself.

Somalis have something for everyone. They have all the fun of an active shorthair cat, but with a long coat. The Somali has all of the luxury of a longhair breed, but without the headache of grooming, as with Persians.

At shows, when spectators ask me what the Somali is like, I say, "Everything that is nice about the Aby is nice about the Somali—the wild look, the disposition . . ."

Most Aby breeders have accepted the Somali today. A few have even sold top-quality Aby kittens to Somali breeders or given Somali females access to their national-winning studs (the offspring of such matings are registered as Somalis). A few Aby breeders still do not accept the existence of the Somali. They have a right to their feelings, so one must not criticize, but the Somali *is* a credit to everything fine and unique in the Aby. In fact, to succeed, a Somali breeder must know the Aby well.

Since that first exciting 1979 championship season, the breed has continued to hold its own in CFA. Nearly a dozen Somalis, both red and ruddy, are now CFA grands.

In 1980-81, Grand Champion Santgria's Coronado, bred and owned by Betty Bridges, was Best National Somali. The same year, my Grand Champion Foxtail's Big Sky became the first Somali to take a "CFA Best of the Bests" win, doing this as Fourth Best of the Best's Kitten. Somalis are now finaling in shows routinely as kittens, adults, and premiers.

The breed also goes about its business in other associations, where it was accepted prior to CFA. The first to recognize the Somali was the Cat Fancier's Federation, Inc. (CFF) in 1975. Then followed the Canadian Cat Association (CCA), Crown Cat Fancier's Federation (CROWN), the United Cat Federa-

Ch. Lapinchat's Sammy Sun of Chapaka. Breeder: Andrea Zaun Balcerski. Owner: Vicki Torrance. This first generation ruddy male is one of the great Somali foundation cats.

A delightful kitten photo of Ch. Foxtail's Krizma of Nephrani. Breeder: Patricia Nell Warren. Owners: Ruth and Bob Morris.

CFA judge Richard Gebhardt handles Lapinchat's Kat Dancer at a 1977 show in Ohio. Breeder: Andrea Zaun Balcerski.

Bahrahman's Rum Tum Toad, a foundation cat, in his Australian "show pen" at a show in New South Wales. Breeder/owner: Mrs. Pat Sheumack.

tion, Inc. (UCF), the American Cat Fanciers' Association, Inc. (ACFA), the American Cat Association, Inc. (ACA), and The International Cat Association (TICA).

Every year, *Cats* magazine lists All-American (AA) show entries by breed, showing a breed's growth (in popularity) rate. For the 1978-79 season, AA Somali entries stood at 259 (roughly one-seventh of the Abys shown that same year) as against 165 for the previous year. The Somali growth rate was a solid 56%. Somali entries dropped for the 1979-1980 season, but so did entries for other breeds, possibly reflecting economic conditions.

Abroad, the Somali is growing in poularity also. Foreign breeders first heard of Somalis through reading U.S. cat magazines. Occasional longhairs have been born to European Abys, and today there are over three dozen breeders of Somalis in Germany, France, Switzerland, Italy, Belgium, and the Netherlands. Countries with no quarantine restrictions have imported some Somalis from the United States. In 1981, the first Somalis went through the three month quarantine in Norway.

In Japan, where longhairs are favored far more than shorthairs, the Somali may be catching on. Japanese Abyssinian breeders already have a number of Somalis from U.S. import lines. Rio's brother, Golden West, granded in Japan under CFA judges.

In Australia, breeders are working with longhairs thrown (produced) by their British-imported Abyssinian lines. Bahrahman Rum Tum Toad, a fine red, is a foundation cat. Due to the lengthy quarantine required on imported cats, no Somalis have arrived from the United States. The breed currently has full recognized status in New South Wales, and work is underway in Queensland.

In England there is great interest, as longhaired Abys have appeared there in years past. In 1981, a consortium of British breeders imported their first pair: a Nephrani male and a Foxtail female. Around 70 people attended the first meeting of the Somali Club of Britain.

As Aby breeders around the world hotly discuss non-standard colors, several blue Somalis are now registered with CFA, although they are not yet recognized for championship status by CFA. These few blue Somalis that are registered are out of Abys who carry both the blue and longhair genes.

Since 1975, the unaffiliated Somali Cat Club of America has given its annual awards, which cover Somalis shown in other countries as well as in Canada and the United States.

The experiences breeding and showing these fine new cats have been unforgettable for all concerned. So "here's to the Somali!" which is just another way of saying, "here's to the Abyssinian, too!"

Gr. Ch. Amulet's Malaika of Anshent-won, D.M., the dam of five grand champions: Anshent-won's Anasazi, Anshent-won's Makeba, Anshent-won's Mesabi, Anshent-won's Maya of Gallantree, and Anshent-won Margaux of Selkhet. Breeder: Elizabeth Freret. Owners: Dr. and Mrs. John W. Boyd (Joyce Chang).

The Cattery Business

by Wain Harding

Many breeders accurately describe the breeding of felines as an expensive hobby. The main reasons for breeding Abyssinians should be a love of the cats and a desire to improve the breed; Abyssinians should not be bred for the purpose of making a profit (many breeders rarely break even, let alone make a healthy profit).

The goal of each cattery should be to produce *quality* cats, not a quantity of cats. Even the most carefully thought-out breeding program will produce many pet-quality kittens, and it is a breeder's responsibility to find loving homes for these kittens. Pet-quality kittens should be sold only with a neuter/spay agreement, and registration papers should *not* be given until the cat is altered. Breeders must make certain that only his or her best kittens are shown and bred.

Breeders will either keep show-quality kittens for breeding and showing or sell them to other responsible breeders. The breeding and showing of cats must go hand in hand. In order to realize the goal of improving the breed, breeders must attend cat shows to see how their Abyssinians stack up against the competition. Breeding and showing Abyssinians can be a fascinating and rewarding hobby if one is willing to invest the required time and money.

Income and Expenses

The largest expense in starting a cattery will be the purchase of the original cat or cats. Most people start with one showable breeder-quality female kitten. She can be shown as a kitten and, hopefully, shown to the title of champion as an adult. This gives the new Abyssinian owner a chance to become familiar with cat shows and to compare the kitten to other Abyssinians being shown.

When the kitten reaches maturity, a suitable mate must be found and arrangements must be made with the owner of the stud cat. In addition to the stud fee, if the stud is not located within driving distance, there will be the additional expense of shipping the queen to him.

The first cattery income usually will occur when your queen's first litter is old enough to go to new homes; however, not all of the money from kitten sales can be considered profit. The breeder may have paid a stud fee, has housed and fed the kittens for three to four months, and has paid for all necessary inoculations and any other veterinary expenses that may have been incurred. Also, if a kitten appears to have show potential, the breeder may have wanted to keep it until it reached six months old or older for the purpose of showing it. A breeder often feels lucky to break even on a litter after all the expenses have been deducted.

When a cattery consists of more than one queen and they have had several litters, the breeder might decide to keep a whole (unaltered) male as a stud cat. It is more difficult to house a stud than it is to keep a queen because most unaltered male cats spray urine to mark their territories. Only top-quality males should be kept and used for breeding. If a breeder buys a potential stud or produces one in a litter, he or she should make sure that it is compatible with the queens in the cattery.

Another possible source of income for a cattery is offering stud service to other breeders. Remember, only a few top examples of a breed are in great demand as studs. These are cats that have excelled in both the show ring and as sires. The owner of the stud must be prepared to screen inquiries to make sure that they are suitable for his or her stud, pick up and deliver queens at the airport, and house the queens while they are visiting. There is always the possibility that a visiting female could injure the stud or bring disease into the cattery. Each cattery must make its own decision on whether or not to give stud service.

There are many other minor and major cattery expenses. There is the day-to-day cost of cat food, vitamin supplements, and cat litter. Many breeders find a large freezer to be a necessity; in order to establish a suitable diet for the cats, raw meat can then be bought in bulk and frozen. A heavy-duty vacuum cleaner makes clean-up chores easier. There is also the cost of routine and emergency veterinary care. Money must be set aside for purchasing cattery cards and pedigree forms, and for advertising. Cat shows are another necessary expense. Breeders must pay for entry fees for each cat, gas and/or plane fare to and from the shows, meals, and motel accommodations, if necessary.

As the cattery population increases, it may become necessary to establish special quarters for the cats. Each cattery will have to meet its own individual needs. If the cattery is limited to two or three queens, a bedroom set aside as a kitten room will be adequate. When the time comes to house a stud cat, more elaborate quarters are necessary. As previously mentioned, most adult male cats spray urine, so they cannot have the run of the house. A room can be remodeled to serve as stud quarters or a large walk-in cage can be built. The place where the stud is kept should be easy to clean and pleasant so he will enjoy living there and his owner will enjoy visiting him. If more than three of four cats are kept, a family room may be remodeled as a cattery.

In order to keep cats healthy and happy, a cattery must have pleasant surroundings, be easy to clean, and be well ventilated. Crowded conditions lead to unhappy cats and, most likely, veterinary bills. A breeder should never keep more cats than he or she can comfortably handle. Remember, Abyssinians are friendly, outgoing cats that require a lot of love and attention.

Cattery Records

A simple but efficient system of recording cattery income and expenses must be established. Each breeder should set up a system with which he or she is comfortable, and records should be kept on a day-to-day basis. If the cattery is set up as a business for tax purposes, the accuracy of these records is doubly important.

A separate record should be maintained on each cat. These can be kept in folders in a file cabinet or in a loose-leaf notebook. This file should contain information on each cat's registration certificate, pedigree, and breeding record. The number of grand champion, regional, and national points should be recorded after each show. Complete health records, including the date of all inoculations and information on any illness, are important to include also.

Information on litters born in the cattery can be placed in the queen's file or each litter can have a file of its own. Litter information should include a pedigree, description of each kitten, and the name and address of the buyer of each kitten.

The Day-To-Day Cattery Notebook

One of the most important cattery records can be kept in a notebook. This is a journal of the day-to-day occurrences in the cattery. Notes are kept on anything out of the ordinary that occurs with the cats. If a cat misses a meal or sneezes excessively, it is recorded in the notebook. A sneeze is usually nothing to worry about, but should the cat become ill, the notebook may contain valuable information for the veterinarian.

Some of the most important information contained in this notebook will be a day-to-day record on the development of each litter of kittens. A physical description of each kitten should be recorded, as well as when the eyes open, when the kittens start eating, and so forth. Each kitten should be weighed and the weight should be recorded daily. Suitable weighing scales can be found in a kitchen supply store. Loss of weight or no gain is often the first sign that all is not well with a kitten. This record may save a kitten's life.

Important information should be transferred from the "day-to-day notebook" to a cat's permanent file.

Abyssinians have become more popular than ever. If your desire is to own one of these intelligent, affectionate, and hauntingly beautiful felines, be prepared to have your name added to the end of a long waiting list.

The Abyssinian Today

The Abyssinian breed is steadily growing in popularity all over the world. More people are selecting them as beautiful, easy-to-care-for, indoor pets. Larger classes appear in the show rings and there are greater numbers of breeders. This popularity boom is inevitable as more people are exposed to the Aby's winning personality and striking appearance.

In order to assess the status of the breed today, a survey of breeders, pet owners, and breed associations was conducted. This was accomplished through private letters, *The Abyssinian Cat Magazine,* and *The Abyssinian Cat Club of America Newsletter*.

Statistical analysis of each question was limited to the *average* of the values which each respondent gave, the *range* from the highest to the lowest answer, the *median* or point at which half of the answers were higher and half of the answers lower, and the *mode* or most common value.

The survey was designed primarily for breeders, and 43 responded. Responses came from all areas of the nation. The states represented were: Alabama, Alaska, California, Illinois, Iowa, Kansas, Kentucky, Maine, Massachusetts, Missouri, Montana, Nevada, New Jersey, New York, North Dakota, Ohio, Oregon, Tennessee, Texas, Virginia, and Washington, plus Washington, D.C.

The Breeder

One of the first areas investigated was the type of person raising Abyssinian cats. Of course, people from all walks of life are involved in breeding, but the following information was distilled:

Age of breeders (years)		Number of years breeding Abys	
Average:	39	Average:	4.1
Median:	33	Median:	3.0
Mode:	31-35	Mode:	3.0
Range:	20-60+	Range:	1-17

169

Number of shows attended in 1978

Average: 12.7
Median: 12.0
Mode: 15.0
Range: 1-40

Number of years showing cats

Average: 7.0
Median: 4.0
Mode: 3.0
Range: 0-34

Number of litters bred in 1978

Average: 2.5
Median: 2.0
Mode: 1.0
Range: 0-9

The average Abyssinian breeder, according to the survey, is female and 39 years of age. She has been breeding Abys for four years and showing them for seven years. She attends 13 shows in a season and breeds three litters per year. However, like all statistical composites, it will be unusual to find anyone who fits this description exactly.

The Number of Abys Entered in United States Shows

The average number of Abys shown in both one- and two-day CFA shows during the 1978 show season was 8.12 cats, according to the CFA central office.

The Number of Abyssinians Registered with CFA

Between 1958 and July, 1979, the following numbers of Abyssinians were registered with the CFA:

		Average number registered per year
Ruddy Males:	5,931	282
Ruddy Females:	8,211	391
Red Males:	520	25
Red Females:	602	27

During the years 1974-1977, these numbers were registered:

		Average number registered per year
Ruddy Males:	1,009	336
Ruddy Females:	2,753	918
Red Males:	273	91
Red Females:	279	93

For the year of 1978, these Abys were registered:

Ruddy Males:	520
Ruddy Females:	799
Red Males:	83
Red Females:	103

A comparison between Abys registered per year for the years 1974-1977 and the year 1978:

184 more Ruddy Males
119 less Ruddy Females
8 less Red Males
10 more Red Females

Net: 67 more Abys registered in 1978 than the average per year between 1974 and 1977.

The Cattery

According to the survey, the breeders own the following number of cats:

Number of queens owned		Number of studs owned	
Average:	3.2	Average:	1.2
Median:	2.0	Median:	1.0
Mode:	2.0	Mode:	1.0
Range:	0-9	Range:	0-5

Thirty-six percent of those who responded own red Abys, and those reds are 11% of the total Aby population represented by the survey.

The percentage of surveyed breeders that also breed other varieties of cats was 25%. These breeds included: Persian, American Shorthair, Siamese, Burmese, Russian Blue, Manx, and Scottish Fold.

The percentage of surveyed breeders that use a neuter/spay agreement was 94.7%. Of these, 65.9% use a written form and 10.5% have an oral agreement with the purchasers of pet kittens. In addition, 62.2% included a requirement that the Aby be kept indoors (written and/or oral).

The survey revealed that 73% of Aby breeders were CFA Breed Council members and that 23.9% were involved in other associations. ACFA and TICA were mentioned the most often.

The way in which breeders classified their kittens varied from person to person; however, some stipulations which were mentioned are listed below. Many breeders indicated it was a difficult task, as kittens could change drastically as they matured. Mistakes had been made, so quite a few people sought opinions from other breeders or judges before making a final decision.

Gr. Ch. Nepenthes Leo, a ruddy male, was a Best Cat in Show winner 30 times. He is the sire of several grand champions. Breeders/owners: Joan and Alfred Wastlhuber.

Pet: Those Abys with one or more disqualifying faults according to the show standard: poor color, thin coat, leg barring, heavy necklace, or incorrect type. In addition, males who were not show quality, cats who would not breed, and cats who could not obtain their championship were classed as pets.

Breeder: Cats without disqualifying faults according to the standard and who have several outstanding features. They will champion but usually not final in the shows. The majority are females. Females are allowed a few poor qualities if they can be overcome by the right stud.

Show: A cat that can easily make its championship, a few finals, and has some potential to grand. It may have minor faults, but overall has excellent qualities.

Top-Show: The Aby who should grand given a chance. It has "pizazz" in addition to excellent conformation.

Most people lost money on their cattery, a few came out even, and several made money. For the majority of breeders, it is an expensive hobby or a losing business.

Health concerns of the cattery varied, but the following were mentioned (in order of frequency):

> upper respiratory infections
> eye problems
> fleas
> FIP
> gingivitis
> diarrhea
> feline acne
> skin problems
> heart disease
> stillbirths
> uterine infections
> hairballs

Kitten Information

A review of 1,500 litters, containing 4,500 Abyssinian kittens, conducted by Tom Dent at CFA produced the following information:

> Average number of kittens per litter: 3
> Percentage of male kittens: 52%
> Percentage of female kittens: 48%

Note: Only living kittens are registered on the litter registration form from which these data were taken.

The survey conducted for this book produced the following data:

Average number of kittens per litter: 3.22
Mode: 4.00
Median: 3.00

Percentage of male kittens: 57.8%
Percentage of female kittens: 42.2%

These results confirm the fact that Abys have small litters. However, the idea that the majority of kittens born are male is probably not true, as the Dent figures indicate the ratio of males to females is virtually fifty-fifty. It may be that some lines produce more males, but overall, the sex ratio appears to be balanced.

According to a 1976 CFA kitten mortality study as reported in *Cat World* magazine (July/August, 1979, p. 50), the number of Abyssinian kittens born alive was 170, with 4 stillborn and 23 dead by one year of age.

In this survey, 325 kittens were reported from 101 litters. Of these kittens, 27 were stillborn (8.3%), 36 died within two weeks (11.1%), and 22 died at from two weeks to 12 weeks (6.8%). Total mortality was 26.2%.

The table below (again, from the CFA study) compares Aby kitten deaths with other breeds.

Gr. Ch. Anshent-won Anahita. Breeders/owners: Dr. and Mrs. John W. Boyd (Joyce Chang).

Total kitten mortality percent by breed for the year 1976

Abyssinian	15%	Japanese Bobtail	21%
American Shorthair	17%	Maine Coon Cat	9%
Balinese	5%	Oriental Shorthair	31%
Birman	16%	Persian	30%
Bombay	39%	Rex	39%
Burmese	38%	Russian Blue	40%
Colorpoint Shorthair	32%	Scottish Fold	40%
Exotic Shorthair	28%	Siamese	31%
Havana Brown	26%	Somali	76%
Himalayan	34%	Turkish Angora	6%

Conclusions

It is hoped that this survey will help readers gain some idea of the status of the Abyssinian breed in the United States today. From information gained through correspondence with breeders throughout the world, it is amazing how similar are the problems and promises of the Abyssinian.

The sample was limited, but perhaps will be expanded by further investigation in the future.

A standard is an esthetic ideal, an objective, something breeders use as they strive to produce the "perfect" cat and something judges use to help them evaluate all of the show cats that they handle in the ring. Like the Aby above, no cat is totally flawless, in terms of the standard, although many come close to perfection.

Interpretation of the Abyssinian Show Standard

by Joan Wastlhuber

Often it has been said that the Abyssinian breed is the most difficult to understand and to judge. At first glance, an Abyssinian appears to be a totally "natural" cat, as most people are immediately taken by its resemblance to a small wild cat. There is a dramatic, striking quality about an Abyssinian; yet, unlike many other breeds, there are no exaggerated features which dominate. Instead, the Aby is made up of numerous complex elements which, when successfully combined, create a balanced and unique look. Although the Aby appears to be "untampered with," years of hard work on the part of serious Abyssinian breeders have gone into maintaining and improving upon this very spontaneous-looking appearance. Even when mating the finest examples of the breed, it is difficult to produce a cat that has all of the components needed to be a top show specimen.

The more judges and Abyssinian breeders become familiar with the breed, the more subtleties they begin to notice. Often it takes many years to fully comprehend the true essence of the Abyssinian. The main purpose of a breed standard is to guide the judges as they attempt to understand the basic qualities which Aby breeders determine to be important in the appearance of the cat. It also establishes the relative importance of these various qualities in comparing one specimen to another. Ideally, a standard should be adequately descriptive yet remain as concise as possible. In order to provide clear criteria for judging, extraneous or superfluous wording is eliminated. Features which are considered attractive are distinguished from those which are vital, and the undesirable characteristics are separated from those which are so severe as to disqualify the cat. Reading the standard alone cannot give a full understanding of the Abyssinian; additionally, considerable knowledge must be gained. To have Abyssinians in one's home and to watch them at cat shows are good ways to start.

The standard sets the criteria for an ideal "perfect" cat. Few, if any, show cats come close to this ultimate goal, and, if they do, there is also the judge's personal interpretation of the standard which must be considered. As more and more Abyssinians are indeed approaching the ideal, breeders have, for several years, been considering some further tightening and clarification of their standard. Each of the American associations has a slightly different standard for show Abyssinians; however, since CFA is the largest registering body of purebred cats in the world, its standard is particularly important to Abyssinian breeders.

CFA STANDARD
ABYSSINIAN

POINT SCORE

HEAD (25)
    Muzzle 6
    Skull 6
    Ears 7
    Eye Shape 6

BODY (30)
    Torso 15
    Legs and Feet 10
    Tail 5

COAT (10)

COLOR (35)
    Color 15
    Ticking 15
    Eye Color 5

In profile, all lines should gently contour, according to the breed standard.

GENERAL: The overall impression of the ideal Abyssinian would be a colorful cat of medium size giving the impression of eager activity and showing a lively interest in all surroundings. Lithe, hard, and muscular. Sound health and general vigor. Well balanced temperamentally and physically; gentle and amenable to handling.

HEAD: A modified, slightly rounded wedge without flat planes; the brow, cheek and profile lines all showing a gentle contour. A slight rise from the bridge of the nose to the forehead, which should be of good size with width between the ears and flowing into the arched neck without a break.

MUZZLE: Not sharply pointed or square. The chin should be neither receding nor protruding. Allowance should be made for jowls in adult males.

176

The dark lidskin, encircled by a light-colored area, is what gives Abyssinians their dramatic look. Gr. Ch. Anshentwon Margaux of Selket. Breeders: Dr. and Mrs. John W. Boyd (Joyce Chang). Owners: Larry and Christel Martin.

EARS: Alert, large, and moderately pointed; broad, and cupped at base and set as though listening. Hairs on ears very short and close-lying, preferably tipped with black or dark brown on a ruddy Abyssinian or chocolate brown on a red Abyssinian.

EYES: Almond-shaped, large, brilliant and expressive. Neither round nor Oriental. Eyes accentuated by dark lidskin, encircled by light-colored area.

BODY: Medium long, lithe and graceful, but showing well-developed muscular strength without coarseness. Abyssinian conformation strikes a medium between the extremes of the cobby and the svelte lengthy type. Proportion and general balance more to be desired than mere size.

LEGS AND FEET: Proportionately slim, fine boned. The Abyssinian stands well off the ground giving the impression of being on tiptoe. Paws small, oval and compact. Toes five in front and four behind.

TAIL: Thick at base, fairly long and tapering.

COAT: Soft, silky, fine in texture, but dense and resilient to the touch with a lustrous sheen. Medium in length but long enough to accommodate two or three bands of ticking.

PENALIZE: Off-Color pads. Long narrow head. Short round head. Barring on legs. Rings on tail. Coldness or grey tones in coat.

DISQUALIFY: White locket, or white anywhere other than nostril, chin, and upper throat area. Kinked or abnormal tail. Dark unbroken necklace. Grey undercoat close to the skin extending throughout a major portion of the body. Any black hair on red Abyssinian. Incorrect number of toes.

ABYSSINIAN COLORS

RUDDY: Coat ruddy brown, ticked with various shades of darker brown or black; the extreme outer tip to be the darkest, with orange-brown undercoat, ruddy to the skin. Darker shading along spine allowed if fully ticked. Tail tipped with black and without rings. The undersides and forelegs (inside) to be a tint to harmonize with the main color. Preference given to unmarked orange-brown (burnt sienna) color. *Nose Leather:* Tile red. *Paw Pads:* Black or brown, with black between toes and extending slightly beyond the paws. *Eye Color:* Gold or green, the more richness and depth of color, the better.

RED: Warm, glowing red, distinctly ticked with chocolate-brown. Deeper shades of red preferred. However, good ticking not to be sacrificed merely for depth of color. Ears and tail tipped with chocolate-brown. *Nose Leather:* Rosy pink. *Paw Pads:* Pink, with chocolate-brown between toes, extending slightly beyond paws. *Eye Color:* Gold or green, the more richness and depth of color, the better.

INTERPRETATION

COLOR

The CFA general description begins by referring to the Abyssinian as a "colorful" cat. This color in the case of a "ruddy" Abyssinian is orange-brown (burnt sienna) in tone with black or dark brown ticking. The deeper shades of orange-brown are the most desired, as long as good brightness and warmth are retained. There should never be a gray or cold tone to the cat's coloring. A dull dark brown impression is also not desired. The sharp contrast of black ticking and tail tip against a brilliant orange-brown background is truly a striking effect.

The "red" Abyssinian is particularly appealing because of its glowing copper-like coloring. The ticking and tail tip are chocolate-brown while the ground color is orange-brown or deep apricot, which gives the cat a beautiful all-over warm red tone. In addition, the red Abys have pink paw pads rather than black or brown and have rosy pink nose leather instead of the deep tile-red of the ruddies. There can be no black hairs anywhere on a red Abyssinian. The body structure and other details of the ruddy and red Abyssinians are to be the same.

All Abyssinians also should have between their toes black fur (brown in the case of the red) which extends slightly beyond the paws. Many years ago, this dark color often extended all the way up to the heels on the hind legs. Although it is rarely seen today, when this does occur, Abyssinian fanciers consider it attractive. There are other details which provide interesting enhancements. Facial markings such as "clown lines" extending from the eyes, dark tufts at the tips of the ears, the slightly darker "eel line" along the spine of the cat, and the narrow stripe which runs up the center of the tail from the small black or brown tip all add character to the overall coloring of the cat.

A very important aspect of the color description in the standard is the emphasis on *unmarked* color. Since the Abyssinian is genetically a variety of tabby, it has taken years of careful selective breeding to eliminate the striping or barring which tends to occur on the legs, chest, shoulders, flanks, and tail. The ideal is complete clarity without any evidence of these tabby markings or any mottling or spotting on the undersides. This is very hard to achieve while still retaining the attractive facial markings as well as the deeper color tones and the strong ticking contrast; however, many truly outstanding examples over the years have proved that it *can* be done. Part of excellence in color is a bright ruddy or orange-brown tone clear "to the skin." As in most wild animal species with ticked fur, there is a tendency for some "gray undercoat" to occur very close to the skin. Abyssinian breeders have chosen to eliminate this, although it is usually tolerated if it is strictly limited to a very small area at the back of the head, neck, and top of the shoulders where the hair is short. When it occurs over a major

Judge Don Swanson checks the shoulders of this entry for gray hair roots. Gray undercoat, when it is found on a major portion of the cat's body, is a serious show fault.

178

portion of the body, it is cause for disqualification in the show ring. Occasionally, this condition is temporary because of an immature kitten coat or it is due to a coat change for various reasons. Judges will inspect beneath the coat to be sure the color is clear, and they will usually fault a cat to some degree if there is evidence of gray undercoat anywhere.

TICKING

One of the most distinctive characteristics of the Abyssinian is its ticked coat. This type of agouti fur is seen in other animal species, including wild rabbits. Each hair has alternating bands of color starting with the clear bright tone at the skin and ending with a dark tip. There must be at least two dark bands on each hair shaft, but some Abyssinians carry more. The ticking covers most of the body but should not extend onto the chest or undersides. A well-ticked Abyssinian coat takes on an iridescent quality when the cat moves, showing flashes of orange color beneath. From a distance it should be easy to distinguish the ticked coat. If the ticking is not distinct enough, the cat will appear solid-colored. If the dark bands are too dominant, the cat will appear very black or dark brown and lack the warm speckled effect over the back and sides. Sometimes there is an unevenness in the banding; this will produce dark and light areas within the ticked coat. It is important that the quality of ticking be just right, as this feature carries many points in the standard. Judges will spend a good deal of time checking this aspect of the cat, sometimes removing several hairs to study them closely.

COAT

The Abyssinian coat texture is also different from that of any other cat. It is soft but not limp or flimsy. When a judge flips back the coat, it resists the hand because of extreme denseness and resiliency and then snaps back into place so that there is no evidence that the cat has even been touched. There is a lustrous sheen and luxurious silky feel to the coat. It lies comfortably over the body, never appearing slick or tight, but also is not bushy or woolly. The medium length is just adequate enough to accommodate the bands of ticking in order to achieve the effect described above. The coats of many breeds of cats are made up of "guard hairs," which are strong shafts to protect the animal from the elements, and also a finer "undercoat" which provides warmth for the cat. In some breeds it is the very soft, fine undercoat which determines the entire coat texture, and there may be a complete absence of guard hairs. In other cats, there is a balance between the two types of soft hair textures. In the Abyssinian breed, it is the guard hairs which dominate. These hairs contain the ticking bands, while the undercoat is shorter, fuzzy in texture, and lacks ticking. The guard hairs have the sheen which gives the lustrous quality called for in the standard. These hairs, because of their

Judge Swanson evaluates his overall impression of entry 29.

179

strength, also provide the resiliency which is necessary without being stiff or coarse. Although some "undercoat" is usually present, if there is too much, the coat may appear bushy. If the guard hairs are too sparse or short, the coat will appear slick and close-lying. Since ten points are allowed for coat texture, it is important that grooming techniques do not damage the hair or change the natural texture. The general health and diet of the cat, as well as weather conditions, also make a difference in the quality of the coat texture.

BODY

Beneath this dense coat, a hard muscular body is apparent even when the cat is viewed from a distance. Abyssinians are surprisingly heavy considering the slim appearance of the body structure. Other cats also have strong muscular bodies, but the Abyssinian displays this well-developed strength without any appearance of coarseness. The body conformation is graceful and lithe rather than chunky or cobby but must not be so fine-boned and svelte as to appear fragile. The contours of the shoulders, torso, rib cage, and hips are slightly rounded, giving a somewhat sculptured look to the body. Every part should be in perfect balance to the whole so that the cat is elegant in its carriage and graceful in its movements. The body length is described as "medium long," which allows the cat to look fluid and ready to spring. The Abyssinian's legs are slim and fine-boned, also in proportion, both in length and substance, to the body. The paws are small, oval, and compact. An Abyssinian has a characteristic stance, often carrying its back in a slightly arched position and raising up as if on tiptoes. Some will pose in this position on the judging stand, displaying unique showmanship. The tail must be thick at the base, fairly long, and tapering without a blunt ending. Occasionally, a judge will check the proper length by bending the tail back to see if the tip will touch the shoulder blades. The overall size of the cat is medium. Overly large Abyssinians sometimes lack the desired graceful appearance, and cats that are too small may not show the regal presence so much a part of the breed. However, the general physical balance and proportion does take precedence over the size of the cat.

HEAD

Perhaps the most expressive part of the Abyssinian is its head. There are no words to fully describe the sweet, alert look of an Abyssinian face. Even though "expression" carries no specific points, it is extremely important. The gentle, intelligent character of an Abyssinian is reflected in its facial components. There should be nothing severe or overbearing in the Abyssinian's head features. The contours of the skull, brow, profile, and cheek are all very slightly curved, forming along with the muzzle a wedge or V-shape. This wedge is described as "modified" because it is not to be excessive or extreme either in length or in form. In contrast to the literal definition of a wedge, there are no flat planes or a sharply pointed ending. A severe indentation, referred to as a "whisker pinch," or a square ending to the muzzle will mar the appearance of the proper modified wedge. Anything which is abrupt disturbs the moderate look desired. A head shape which is round or short cannot fit the wedge description. When the head is viewed from the side, the profile begins with a level nose and rises in a gradual curve from the bridge of the nose to the forehead without a stop or "break." The line continues, slightly curving over the forehead and skull and flowing into the neck, which is carried in an arched position. The jaw line and moderately full chin, which neither protrudes nor recedes, carries out the contours of the muzzle. The ears are the elements which finish off the head form. They are placed in line with the modified wedge shape of the head and appear as much on the side of the head as on the top when viewed from the front. Abyssinian ears are prominent, which contributes a great deal to the overall alert expression. They are large and arched forward as though listening. The base is broad and cupped, and the outer line is slightly curved to form a moderately pointed ending. Narrow ears with straight lines and sharply pointed at the tip are not considered to be proper for an Abyssinian no matter how large.

The eyes are especially expressive because of their large size and brilliant color. The standard calls for either gold or green. The gold can range from yellow tones through the almost orange/amber eye shades. All are acceptable if they are deep and rich. True green-eyed Abys are unusual today; however, if the color is brilliant emerald, it is an extremely striking contrast to the bright orange-brown coat color. The eyes are accentuated even further by the dark lidskin and light-colored fur encircling them. The proper shape is exactly that of an almond nut—very broad and tapering at the outer end. Eyes which are round or oval in shape, slanted, or narrow do not fit the pure almond form called for. When the shape, set, and color are right, the Abyssinian's eyes look gentle, bright, and inquisitive.

PENALIZE AND DISQUALIFY

The ideal Abyssinian should have all the features described in the standard. However, since each cat will probably have some flaws, the "penalize" section of the standard points out those which are especially severe. When these particular faults are present, they count heavily against a cat which otherwise may be good, and a judge may withhold wins from a cat displaying these faults.

Those faults listed under "disqualify" are totally unacceptable in a show Abyssinian. When any one of these occurs, the judge should not award any ribbons at all. A white "locket" is a spot occurring on the chest or throat surrounded by the ground color. White may be around the nostrils, on the chin, and on

Assessing skull shape and profile.

the *upper* throat area only. Most people prefer the chin to be white or light cream as this adds to the mountain lion look of the face. However, if pure white extends below the "Adam's apple" in the throat, it is usually considered to be too low. A line of white dropping below the upper throat is called a "drip" or "extension" and is also not allowed. Other areas of the body where white spotting will sometimes occur are in the arm pits, on the belly, and in the groin area. A tail abnormality is often very difficult to detect on any Abyssinian since obvious visible kinks are rare. The most common abnormalities occur near the end of the tail and especially at the tip, where the last vertebrae may be sharply angled, end with a knob, or be missing altogether. The most recent addition to the DISQUALIFY Section concerns gray undercoat.

The desired visual characteristics of the Abyssinian have changed very little over the years. Abyssinian breeders today, as in the past, are highly protective of their breed. Conscientious selection of breeding cats and careful placement of kittens, which have show faults, as pets (with altering agreements) have kept the general quality of the breed high.

It is interesting to compare some of the comments made by Mr. H.C. Brooke, a prominent English Abyssinian breeder of 50 years ago, with the current standard. In his article "The Abyssinian Cat," published April, 1929, by the *Somerset Country Gazette,* Taunton, England, Mr. Brooke describes, in part, the characteristics of the breed:

> The general appearance of the Abyssinian is that of a rather small and very elegantly built cat, with graceful slender limbs, elegant head, with rather large ears and lustrous eyes. What is commonly called in the Fancy the "British type" is here out of place; we do not want round short head, small ears, cobby build and powerful limbs. The most usual colour of the Abyssinian very strikingly resembles that of a wild rabbit, when placed side by side, until carefully examined, when it is seen that the fur of the rabbit is grey near the skin (under colour) whilst that of the cat is, or should be rufous. The "ticking" is a most essential property of the Abyssinian, and is caused by blackish, or dark brown, tips to the hair. Some— the best ticked—have about three-quarters of the length of each hair rufous, then two or three bands of brown or orange or orange shades, the darkest being at the tip . . . the under colour should always be as bright and clear as possible, not a dull lifeless brown, which much detracts from the beauty of the cat . . . Absence of markings, i.e. bars on head, tail, face and chest is a very important property in this breed . . . The belly fur is not ticked as on the rest of the body, and should be free from spots or stripes; the colour should be a light brown, matching the

Above and below: Judge Ricky Carroll checks the throat area for lockets, necklace, and color.

Cat shows are a great place to meet and talk with breeders and to see some of the finest representatives of the Abyssinian breed, as well as other breeds. Study the Aby breed standard and observe the judging process to see firsthand what judges look for in a cat.

other parts . . . A little black tail tip seems to me to give a nice finish; the heels are also black. Ears large and open, and a blackish or dark brown tip to the ears is desirable. The head looks slender and pointed, but not of the wedge-shape or "marten-face" sought for in the Siamese . . . Eyes: These should be large and lustrous, of kind expression; more oval than in the "British" cat. As regards colour, I prefer a bright green, personally, but a nice amber eye is certainly preferable to a "greenery-yallery, washed out" looking eye. White marks of any kind such as on chest, throat, or toes, taboo in show specimens . . . In short, it is one of the most charming and interesting varieties we have, and it has time and again been shown that a really good Abyssinian can usually be relied upon to do pretty well when it comes to judging the "mixed special prizes" at shows.

Aside from the specific requirements outlined by the CFA standard for the Abyssinian, there are some general "condition" requirements which are important in the judge's evaluation of show cats, and which apply equally to all of the breeds. A show cat must be "in prime physical condition," with the proper weight, giving the appearance of "general health and vigor," and be "faultlessly clean" and well groomed. The temperament reflects a "stable disposition," and the cat must be amenable to handling. It is not enough to present a cat which meets the standard for the individual parts. All of the parts must fit together so that the "total cat" looks and feels balanced. In addition, the cat should be "receptive to the judging procedure" and give an extra effort to "exhibit the characteristic grace and beauty natural to its breed." This is the elusive but important aspect of showmanship which, when everything else is there, will give a cat that special edge in the show ring.

A EUROPEAN STANDARD
Governing Council of the Cat Fancy
(GCCF)

SCALE OF POINTS

COLOUR
Body colour 25
Ticking 20

TYPE
Body shape, tail, feet, coat,
carriage, and general 30
Head and ears 15
Eyes 10

TOTAL   100

ABYSSINIAN-VARIETIES 23, 23a, and 23b

Type: Foreign type of medium build, firm, lithe and muscular, never large or coarse. The head to be broad and tapering to a firm wedge set on an elegant neck. The body to be of medium length with fairly long tapering tail. A "cobby" cat is not permissible.

Head and Ears: Head is a moderate wedge of medium proportions, the brow, cheeks and profile lines showing a gentle contour and the muzzle not sharply pointed. A shallow indentation forming the muzzle is desirable but a pinch is a fault. Ears set wide apart and pricked, broad at base, comparatively large, well cupped and preferably tufted. In profile the head shows a gentle rounding to the brow with a slight nose-break leading to a very firm chin.

Eyes: Well apart, large, bright and expressive in an oriental setting. A squint is a fault. Colour, amber, hazel or green. A light eye colour is undesirable.

Tail: Broad at base, fairly long and tapering. Neither a whip nor a kink is permissible.

Feet: Small and oval.

Coat: Short, fine and close lying with double, or preferably, treble ticking, i.e., two or three bands of colour on each hair.

Markings: It is required that the appropriate darker hair colour extends well up the back of the hind legs; also showing as a solid tip at the extreme end of the tail, and the absence of either is a fault. A line of dark pigmentation is required round the eyes and absence of this is also a fault.

Undesirable markings are bars on the legs, chest and tail. An unbroken necklet is not permissible. The Abyssinian cat has a tendency to white in the immediate area of the lips and lower jaw and it is a fault if this white area extends onto the neck. A locket and other white markings are not permissible.

COLOURS

USUAL-VARIETY 23

The body colour to be a rich golden brown, ticked with black and the base hair ruddy-orange or rich apricot. A pale or cold colour is a fault.

The belly and inside of legs to be a ruddy-orange or rich apricot to harmonize with the base hair on the rest of the body. Any spinal shading to be of deeper colour. The tip of the tail and the solid colour on the hind legs to be black. Nose leather to be brick red and pads to be black.

RED-VARIETY 23a

The body colour to be a lustrous copper-red, ticked with chocolate and the base hair deep apricot. A pale or sandy colour is a fault.

The belly and inside of legs to be a deep apricot to harmonize with the base hair on the rest of the body. Any spinal shading to be of deeper colour. The tip of the tail and the solid colour on the hind legs to be chocolate. Nose leather and pads to be pink.

BLUE-VARIETY 23c (Provisional Standard)

The body colour to be blue-grey with a soft warm effect, ticked with deeper steel blue and the base hair pale cream or oatmeal.

The belly and inside of legs to be pale cream or oatmeal to harmonize with the base hair on the rest of the body. Any spinal shading to be of deeper colour. The tip of the tail and the solid colour on the hind legs to be steel blue. Nose leather to be dark pink and pads to be mauve/blue.

Note: Any cat displaying a feature which is not permissible (i.e., cobby type; whip tail, kink in tail; unbroken necklet; locket; other white markings) shall not be awarded a first prize, or a challenge certificate or a premier certificate.

Any cat displaying a fault may be awarded a prize but any cat displaying two or more faults shall not be awarded a challenge certificate or a premier certificate.

From: The Abyssinian Breeders International Year Book 1976, published privately.

REFERENCES IN THE TEXT

Aronson, A.L., "Diseases Caused by Chemical and Physical Agents," *Feline Medicine and Surgery*, 2nd Ed., Catcott, E.J., Ed., American Veterinary Publications, 1975, p. 125.

Beaver, Bonnie, D.V.M., "Feline Behavioral Problems," *Veterinary Clinics of North America*, 6 (3):333-340, August, 1976.

Collins, D.R., "Dietary Consideration in Feline Practice," *Veterinary Clinics of North America*, 6 (3):341-352, August, 1976.

Denham, Helen and Sidney Denham, *Child of The Gods*, H. Denham, London, 1951.

Fairchild, L.H., M.D., and Helen Fairchild, *Cats and All About Them*, Orange Judd Publishing Co., Inc., 1955.

Gardner, Eldon J., *Principles of Genetics*, John Wiley and Sons, Inc., New York, 1972, pp. 403-424.

Hart, Benjamin, D.V.M., "Aggression In Cats," *Feline Practice*, 7 (2):22, 24, 28, March, 1977.

Hart, Benjamin, D.V.M., "Problem Solving," *Feline Practice*, 9 (1):9-10, January-February, 1979.

Oliphant, F.J. and J.D. Tovey, "Water Balance Studies in Domestic Cats," *Feline Practice*, 7 (4):30-33, July, 1977.

Pederson, Niels C., "Feline Infectious Diseases," Seminar presented to the Central Arizona Veterinary Medical Association, June, 1979, Tempe, Arizona.

Scott, F.W., et al., "Kitten Mortality Complex (Neonatal FIP?)," *Feline Practice*, 9 (2):44-56, March-April, 1979.

Volmer, Peter J., "Feline Inappropriate Elimination," *Veterinary Medical/Small Animal Clinician*, Part I, June 1979, pp. 796-797; Part II, July 1979, pp. 928-929; Part III, August 1979, pp. 1101-1102.

Zanetti, Aida, Elinor Dennis, and Mary Hantzmon, *Journey from the Blue Nile*, The United Abyssinian Club, Inc., New York, 1960.

FURTHER READING

Anon., *The Borden Guide for the Care and Feeding of Orphan and Rejected Kittens*, Borden Chemical, Norfolk, Virginia.

Carr, William H.A., *The Basic Book of the Cat*, Gramercy Publishing Co., New York, 1971.

Catcott, E.J., *Feline Medicine and Surgery*, 2nd Ed., American Veterinary Publications, Inc., Santa Barbara, California, 1975.

Collins, D.R., "The 'All Meat' Syndrome," *Current Veterinary Therapy, Small Animal Practice*, W.B. Saunders Co., 1974, pp. 85-87.

Cotter, S.M., "Feline Leukemia Virus Induced Disorders in the Cat," *Veterinary Clinics of North America*, 6 (3):367-374, August, 1976.

Doering, G.G. "Feline Dermatology," *Veterinary Clinics of North America*, 6 (3):463-477, August, 1976.

Duch, D.S. and D.W. Hammar, "The Effect of Body Weight and Castration on the Occurrence of the Feline Urologic Syndrome," *Feline Practice*, 8 (6):35-40, November, 1978.

Field, Edna, "Red Abys," *1967 CFA Yearbook*.

Ford, R.B., "Feline Viral Respiratory Disease: Current Concepts," *The Compendium on Continuing Education*, 1 (5):337-343, May, 1979.

Gershoff, S.N., "Nutritional Requirements of Cats," *Gaines Dog Research Progress*, Winter, 1964-65.

Gorham, J.R., F.B. Henson, and C.J. Dodgen, "Basic Principles of Immunity in Cats," *Journal of the American Veterinary Medical Association*, 158 (6): 846-853, March, 1971.

Green, Earl (Ed.), *Biology of The Laboratory Mouse*, McGraw-Hill Book Co., New York, 1966.

Hatez, E.S.E., *Reproduction in Farm Animals*, Lea & Febiger, Philadelphia, 1974.

Hathaway, J.E., "Feline Anemia," *Veterinary Clinics of North America*, 6 (3):495-510, August, 1976.

Five-month-old Avenue Isadora of Nepenthes. Breeders: Duane and Hertha Chellevold. Owners: Joan and Alfred Wastlhuber.

Ing, Catherine and Grace Pond, *Champion Cats of the World*, St. Martins Press, Inc., 1972.

Joshua, J.O., "Feline Geriatrics," *Journal of Small Animal Practice*, 5 (6):525-534, 1964.

Jude, A.C., *Cat Genetics*, T.F.H. Publications, Inc., Neptune, New Jersey, 1967.

Kahn, D.E. and E.A. Hoover, "Infectious Respiratory Diseases of Cats," *Veterinary Clinics of North America*, 6 (3):399-414, August, 1976.

Kallfelz, Francis A., "Notes on Feline Nutrition," Northwest Feline Research Group, Seattle, Washington, July, 1979.

Kirk, R.W. (Ed.), *Current Veterinary Therapy IV, Small Animal Practice*, W.B. Saunders, 1974.

Lautenslager, J.P., "Internal Helminths," *Veterinary Clinics of North America*, 6 (3):353-366, August, 1976.

Lewis, Lon D., "Feeding and Care of the Cat," *Cat World*, 7 (3):18-22, July/August, 1979.

Loeffler, D.G., et al., "The Incidence of Naturally Occurring Antibodies Against Feline Infectious Peritonitis in Selected Cat Populations," *Feline Practice*, 8 (1): 43-47, January, 1978.

Miller, Richard, "Selecting Breeding Stock for your Cattery," *Feline Science*, 1(2), July, 1979.

Oliphant, F.J., "Nutritional Requirements of Cats," *J. So. Afr. V.M.A.*, 39(4):18-24, 1968.

Peltz, Rosemonde, "The Abyssinian Cat," *1972 CFA Yearbook*, reprinted 1973 by TEX-ABY Club, Houston, Texas.

Robinson, Roy, *Genetics for Cat Breeders*, Pergamon Press, New York, 1977.

Scott, F.J., "Current Concepts in Feline Infectious Peritonitis," Presented at American Veterinary Medical Convention, Seattle, Washington, July, 1979.

Scott, F.W. and R. Peltz, "Kitten Mortality Survey," *Feline Practice*, 8(6), November, 1978.

Scott, P.P., "Nutrition and Disease," *Feline Medicine and Surgery*, 2nd Ed., Catcott, E.J., Ed., American Veterinary Publications, 1975, pp. 131-144.

Shaw, Don, "Diluter Systems and the Abyssinian—Are all Abys genetically the same or are there two different kinds?" *All Pets*, July, 1964, pp. 5-7.

Shaw, Don, "Is the Red Abyssinian Really Red?" *Cats*, March, 1977, pp. 23, 27-28.

Sherding, R.G., "Feline Infectious Peritonitis," *Compendium of Continuing Education*, 1(2):95-101, February, 1979.

Timoney, J.F., "Toxoplasmosis," *Veterinary Clinics of North America*, 6(3):379-384, August, 1976.

Todd, J.D., "Immune Response to Parenteral and Intranasal Vaccinations," *J.A.V.M.A.*, 163(7):807-809, October, 1973.

Wolfgang, Harriet, *Short Haired Cats*, T.F.H. Publications, Inc., Neptune, New Jersey, 1963.

Also:

ACCA Newsletter, especially September, 1979.

CFA Yearbooks, 1967-date.

Index